EXCERPT FROM A REVIEW
by Mel Keegan of GLBT Bookshelf

ODD GIRL REVISITED is a work of 'rare scholarship'-- so much so that it's not the "easy read" the mass market is looking for these days. It's a window on a world which is gone, and the savvy reader's brows will be popping up in many places, for many reasons ... as much an invaluable glimpse into its times as into the lives and hearts of gay/Gay girls who grew up in the decades before most of us were born.)

The strength of the book is in its "realness." And I know that's not a word; but it's what I want to say. The people, places and events in this book are real. Fantastic as it seems (and the first 20pp, the backstory of the author's childhood, do seem more in keeping with a big-budget HBO Movie of the Week!) these events took place. As the Chinese curse goes, "May you live in interesting times." ...

Recommended for the well-read; for the reader who isn't using the encyclopedia to prop up the DVD stand; for the writer researching the period'-- with or without any interest in gay culture of the twentieth century. Ideally suited to the American social and cultural studies, and of great interest as a window on the recent past. Also should catch the attention of executives at HBO, who might easily be captivated with the first 20pp, buy the movie rights and never even read the rest of the book! (One can see it now, starring Meryl Streep, Cate Blanchett, Sam Neill and Viggo Mortensen...)

--BookWorld.editme.com GLBT Bookshelf,
December 6, 2010

ArtemisSmith's ODD GIRL *Revisited*

Previous publications: LCN 2010915235, LCN 2010916162
"ArtemisSmith's **Odd Girl Revisited" by ArtemisSmith**
© 2010 by The Savant Garde Institute. All rights reserved.

ABRIDGED REVISED MASS MARKET EDITION
"ArtemisSmith's **Odd Girl Revisited"**
© 2011 by The Savant Garde Institute. All rights reserved.
ISBN 978-1-878998-35-4

(Also available as an 8.5x11 book art edition under
Library of Congress Control No: 2011920574
Order direct from Publisher, numbered and author-thumbprinted.
Retail Price: $500 + custom binding ISBN 9781878998361)

'the savant garde workshop' publishers:
P.O. Box 1650 . Sag Harbor . NY 11963-0060 . USA
Tel/fax: 1-631-725-1414

Since 1954 Artemis Smith has been a pen name for
Baroness Annselm L.N.V. Morpurgo, MA, CPC

ArtemisSmith's ODD GIRL *Revisited*

ArtemisSmith's ODD GIRL *Revisited*
an autobiographical correlate

Portrait of Artemis Smith by Billie Taulman 1955

a *Monograph of*
THE SAVANT GARDE INSTITUTE

ArtemisSmith's ODD GIRL *Revisited*

To
Vilna Jorgen Morpurgo
Attilio Giacomo Morpurgo, M.D.
and
Billie Ann Taulman

ArtemisSmith's ODD GIRL *Revisited*

Dear Colleagues:

The work titled by my publishers *Odd Girl* (© 1959) and by me "Anne Loves Beth," while based upon real first-hand experiences which I enjoyed and lived through with adolescent abandon, was strictly a work of fiction.

Those of you who have read many of my works have come to realize that it is impossible to confuse me with any of my characters. It is the task of every accomplished fiction writer to always appear to be telling a true story.

But if it is authentically to be a work of art, the story must ring true -- the details must be seen as merely composites of various aspects of the author's vastly wider self -- or else, it would not be possible for the story to be written at all!

ArtemisSmith's ODD GIRL *Revisited*

Who am I, what am I? *Really?*

Unlike my character Anne, who was sculpted as born of modest folk, my own roots are royal and my artistic ambitions are world-historical. On both sides of my family I come from a long line of movers and shakers, and from the start I was raised to take my rightful place among them.

If this sounds elitist and contemptuous, live with it!

It's time to call an end to the *rights* cult of the inept and the drug culture that has given rise to it. All true master-builders are natural-born aristocrats and this Jeffersonian ideal is open to anyone who has the *cohunes* to seriously apply.

This is how I have lived my life and wish to be remembered:

> *Don't limit me. I am neither "Gay/gay," nor "Lesbian/lesbian," neither male nor female but wholly unisex, unirace, gender-free.*

If you prefer, you can modernize this to read *post-ethnic*, *post-racial* and *post-gender* (not to be confused with t*ransgende*r, a very opposite term which I do not endorse).

Most importantly, I have never been a hack and I most emphatically never wrote "Anne Loves Beth" for hire to the pulp fiction trade. It was simply my first mass market offering, an early attempt at activist cultural change, and no establishment publisher would touch it.

All the more reason to get it into print. Give it to the yellow sheets if I must, but get the world-shaking message through!

Nearly sixty years later I still stand defiant, a cultural-guerrilla born of a long line of cultural-guerrillas – artists and philosophers all unisex and unirace, none of them decadent, all of them aristocrats.

To better know me you will have to read my web-interactive picture memoir, *PteroDARKtyl*. But here I will offer you a quick peek: at me, my family, my closest friends, and the intolerable socio-political climate that prompted the writing of *Odd Girl,* originally titled "Anne Loves Beth."

Perhaps then you will understand why the work had to be written as a genuinely activist work of art, of cultural master-building; and why I, of political necessity, finally allowed the highly inferior first draft to be promoted throughout the gay activist community despite the existence of a more polished and mature version of the original manuscript - for it is unlikely that the finished manuscript, innocent as it was by modern standards, would ever have passed the censors back in the 1950's or '60's.

[And be certain not to skip the footnotes, which for easier reading I have in this edition inserted inside the main narrative in an alternate typeface! Would that the printed page could be as large and wide as a tabloid so that you might skim over a lot of it at once and focus on what you please!]

I completed the first draft of "Anne Loves Beth" known to lesbiana aficionados as *Odd Girl* in 1953. As previously said, the work was not strictly autobiographical. The places and characters are all composites, and like all my leading ladies, Anne -while encompassing many of my adolescent feelings and emotions - is not really anything like me. Nor is her family anything like mine: I was born in Rome, Italy, and chaotically raised in a palatial setting by Catholic servants - some of whom affectionately (and others not quite so fondly) referred to me as their *baronina* (Little Baroness).

But this palazzo was only one of my homes.

Two years after I was born I had been left there in foster care at my recently-widowed American-born Sephardic Freemason grandmother's house while my Scandinavian mother, a well-known artist and journalist, was wrestling with her conscience, trying to decide whether to abandon me to an increasingly Zionist household or snatch me away and take both me and my younger sister Helga back to Sweden with her.

[My grandmother Ida Olga DeCastro-Morpurgo-Sierra-Morpurgo-Morpurgo was born in the USA, probably on Staten Island, and kin to Emma Lazarus. Most Morpurgos married cousins and were multiple-cousins, and their progeny were quasi-clones, often dropping the surname in favor of paternal middle-names, e.g., Lazzaro, Lazard, Lazarus. And to make matters even more confusing, the surname changed with each locality, so you can also call us Marpurg, Marburg, Marlborough or Murphy.]

Two years earlier there may have been confusion over which of Ida's sons, Aldo or Attilio, was my biological father and should be laying claim to me.

Vilna was temperamentally closer to my architect uncle Aldo who was collaborating with her on public monuments commissioned by Mussolini.

Aldo might have been Vilna's first choice, but as the oldest son expected to preserve the family name and fortune, he had been already engaged sight-unseen to my ashkinazi aunt Valentina D'Arton arriving from Cairo, half her lavish dowry already having been received and expended. That had only left Aldo's younger brother Attilio, who was also dating Vilna and was also completely mesmerized by her Garboesque stature and her Isadora style.

(Or perhaps Vilna had simply decided to marry freemason Attilio, who was not circumcised, and did not want to be circumcised and become a Zionist, and who continued to be madly in love with her for the rest of his life. Whatever the reason, two years earlier Vilna had been pregnant and had to either marry or abort and, once married, had still remained uncertain about her future since she definitely had no intention of converting to Judaism.

[Vilna, three years older than Attilio, was a widow from a previous marriage most likely to the real great love of her life, a Norwegian named Jorgensen - but she never spoke of him until we were fully grown.]

Valentina, an immensely intelligent, worldly and mature woman, had been raised in a Moslem state where polygamy and communal child-rearing was the norm. Given the situation, she was more than anxious to adopt me and raise me as her own, but she was also hell-bent on converting and taking the whole family back to Egypt for Jewish "repatriation" in the Palestinian "Promised Land."

Vilna would also have been welcome, but she would have to convert along with Ida and Attilio, and both Aldo and Attilio would have to be circumcised so that the children would all be accepted as legitimate Jews.

Vilna totally recoiled.

A contract being a contract, Aldo and Ida stoically complied.

Attilio was split between loyalty to Vilna and loyalty to mother and brother. Vilna, furious with him, was threatening to divorce and leave one child behind. But which child? The Germanic blonde one claimed by Attilio who looked more like many Morpurgo Austrian cousins or the dark one, who looked more Scandinavian but was claimed by Ida, Aldo and now also Valentina?

Vilna couldn't make up her mind.

Now came the clash between Vilna's Scandinavian Feminism and Valentina's increasingly imposed Ashkinazi Traditionalist tyranny over the Roman Catholic servants at Ida's Sephardic Freemason household.

Vilna had named me after my grandfather Anselmo, whom she adored. He had just died before I was born and both Ida and Vilna wanted me to be raised to be just like him. I assumed that meant I was their son since I had never been explicitly told I was a girl until Valentina's son was born, when in the care of the servants I suffered an extreme shock of conflicting gender identity and a classic case of penis envy.

The servants, now also receiving advice from their parish priest as to how to properly raise two newly-baptized Catholic-Hebrews, had become thoroughly confused as to whose instructions they should obey and resorted to doing their best to persuade me that little girls were created *after* little boys and consequently were not as important in God's eyes as little boys and should accept their inferiority and lack of a penis.

Meanwhile Valentina, having been raised in Egypt and now speaking in either English or French or Italian, got most of what she meant lost in translation. Hypocritical linguistic conventions that gave lip service to the inferiority of women even while masking an ironic inner dialogue of feminine contempt were by me taken literally. In truth it was the men in our household who were totally hen-pecked, but Valentina's chiding manner was most foreign and grotesque and to my three-year-old ears entirely enraging - as was the gender-rich Italian language which divided all the world's objects into the strong and the weak.

I was *not* anyone's girl-child, I was *not* inferior! *I* was the eldest, *I* was the stronger, *I* was the one to inherit and defend the Morpurgo name.

Valentina's bell-ringing by-the-book state of the art child-rearing (Pavlov was the new rage) didn't help either. Both I and Helga were soon reduced to tantrums and screams.

The servants were helpless.
Ida was helpless.
Aldo and Attilio were hiding.
Vilna suddenly heard.

Sexual politics really may finally have decided the issue: our Viking mother, herself raised as gender-free, could not bear to abandon either infant to

Valentina's newly-imposed now also Pavlovian Traditionalism or the servant's Roman-Catholicism.

No daughter of hers would *ever* be raised as inferior and subservient to *any* man. Hearing our cries and despising all Valentina's ways, Vilna angrily declared both of her children *hers* and snatched us back.

But this is putting things a little too simply. Vilna, as a teen-aged victim of a broken marriage, and as the eldest half-sister, had already raised two huge litters of siblings before she ran away from both Sweden and Norway. She was demanding more servants be hired to take care of them. But money was now tight. Ida's staff was reduced to two spinster sisters who had raised Aldo and Attilio: Lucia who cooked all day, and overloaded Amabile who did everything else and came up short.

ArtemisSmith's ODD GIRL *Revisited*

Dear Colleagues:

My artist-journalist mother had already lived a full life before she gave birth to me. She had danced with Nijinsky at the Royal Ballet of Sweden where Garbo had been a classmate. She had run away from both parents of a broken marriage at the age of sixteen and supported herself as a foreign correspondent on assignment from *Bonniers,* and by sculpting the portraits of many children of Norwegian, Swedish, Danish and Belgian royal families where her mother, a social butterfly and frequent "Lady in Waiting," had once presented her to the various monarchs, herself being a Royal. While in Oslo at her father's house [Jarl (Earl) Adolphe Martinius Nilsen], Vilna had interviewed Trotsky and became fired with Bolshevism, then had trekked by caribou-sleigh and overland skis up through Finland and down by rail through Northern Russia and Czechoslovakia, all the way covering the ripples of the Revolution. En route she married fellow journalist, Karlssen Jorgensen, and they reached Prague, Berlin, then Paris where they lived on the Left Bank.

ArtemisSmith's ODD GIRL *Revisited*

Together they starved in the proverbial garret while he slowly wasted of TB. Supporting both of them with her writing, art work and professional dancing, Vilna performed the Tango and Flamenco (but refused to dance the Apache because it was too demeaning to women) at classy Parisian night spots as part of a Spanish troupe and exhibited alongside the post-Impressionists in the famed street show known as the Paris *La Horde*.

At thirty and now a grief-stricken widow, Vilna tagged along with the Spaniards to Barcelona and was simultaneously commissioned to cover and represent Norway in an international art exposition cancelled by the thermidor of the Spanish Civil War.

Not staying for the action, she hitched a ride in one of the first airmail carriers and nearly crashed-landed in Rome where, thanks to both the Swedish and Norwegian Ambassadors, she immediately found work as a royal portrait sculptor and Vatican forger and restorer.

[Upon the recommendation of the Scandinavian Consuls, the Italian *Imperatrice* commissioned her to sculpt the royal children. Vilna referred to it as really a glorified job of Royal kindergarten art teaching and baby-sitting. Go to http://vilnajorgen.tripod.com/VilnaBio.html]

Exhibiting in galleries in Via Flaminia, she came to share a studio on Via Marghutta with Baroness Clarissa von Blumenthal, a Weimar post-Impressionist/Expressionist who taught Vilna, then mostly only a sculptor, to paint like Rembrandt. At von Blumenthal's Vilna met my uncle Aldo and my father

ArtemisSmith's ODD GIRL *Revisited*

Attilio.

Prior to 1937, Aldo Morpurgo was Mussolini's favorite architect and commissioned Vilna to work with him on a number of public projects. Either he or von Blumenthal introduced her to IL Duce.

[Architectural chronicler Richard Meier appears to refer to him as Franco Morpurgo, but that must be either a Fascist redo or a hyphenated signature, or Aldo's middle name.]

But by 1937, Mussolini - anxious to imitate Hitler and bring Scandinavians into the Axis side - declared Vilna his favorite portrait artist and ordered her to do his bust with that of Hitler. Unable to refuse without risking the immediate arrest of her entire family, she fulfilled the commission then took a hammer and destroyed the work, declaring it artistically inferior and not suitable for showing.

By then she had decided to keep both of her children and stay married to Attilio and we were all desperately trying to get out of town.

Lucia and Amabile with Helga c. 1938. When we fled Italy they retired to Tuscany with all the family's centuries-old Sephardic recipes as a parting gift from Ida, now famous on the internet as *La Cucina Morpurgo de Nilma*. Photo by four-year-old Annaselma.

ArtemisSmith's ODD GIRL *Revisited*

Dear Colleagues:

Thanks to Vilna the entire family escaped the Holocaust and our side emigrated to the USA in June 1940, in one of the last two passenger ships allowed past the British blockade at Gibraltar. Vilna had a visa to represent Norway at the New York World's Fair and we were all set to jump ship once we got there - but at the last moment, due to the efforts of an American-Jewish lady later identified as Lillian Hellman, our immigration papers came through.

But now let me properly introduce my father, Baron-Doctor Attilio Giacomo Morpurgo, who was a prominent physician and best friend and closest school chum of Enrico Fermi. Attilio was the only one of his school chums who didn't think Fermi was retarded. That was why they grew up as best friends. They were very much alike, looked alike.

[Fermi used to play with me when I was one or two or three and four and taught me how to judge distance and perspective in a mirror, declaring me a genius for comprehending the concept almost immediately.]

ArtemisSmith's ODD GIRL *Revisited*

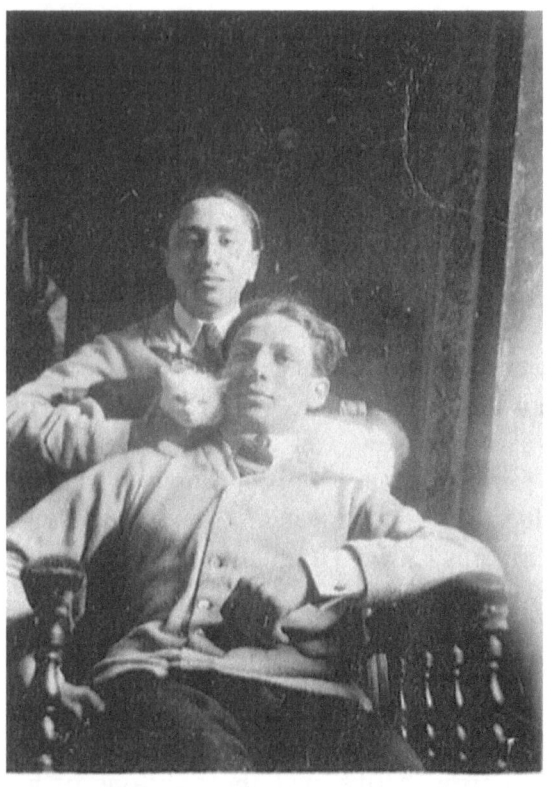

Attilio Morpurgo and Enrico Fermi and our cat, Mimi, at our NYC apartment c. 1942. Photo by Vilna Jorgen Morpurgo.

[When Fermi visited us c. 1942, he laughingly told us how it had taken the entire State Department to convince the Immigration authorities at Ellis not to send him back for failing an elementary intelligence test!]

ArtemisSmith's ODD GIRL *Revisited*

Attilio was a very mild, gentle - some persons would say *feminine* man - but a top-notch internist and diagnostician who identified and successfully contained many diphtheria epidemics in fascist youth camps during his military service. This had won him fame and promotions until Mussolini fired him as an "Italian Jew." By then he held the post of *Assistente Primario* of the United Hospitals of Rome - a position comparable to Deputy Surgeon General.

But in the USA Attilio was just another dark-skinned not-very-Jewish Italian-Egyptian refugee needing to go back to medical school to get his license to practice in New York. He spent his first year of internship at Welfare Island Hospital (now called Roosevelt Island but once a place for infectious diseases where Typhoid Mary lived and died) either running the elevator or cutting up corpses.

[All of this has important bearing on my own academic and political career in the late 1960's and early '70's when, upon new recommendation for a career post, my background in the civil rights movements collided with the Secret Service and with a maelstrom of forces unleashed by the infiltration of the FBI and CIA by the Mafia and the Noriega Drug Cartels, further infiltrating the R.O.T.C., under the tenure of then-CIA-head George H.W. Bush. Does it sound like a Salsa? Yes, it does; It should all make sense later.]

ArtemisSmith's ODD GIRL *Revisited*

"The Manhattan Project" c. 1943. Attilio is the little guy holding the pipe.

ArtemisSmith's ODD GIRL *Revisited*

Dr. Henry Kissinger happened to be an administrator there and this marked a fortuitous moment for many, for when Fermi arrived in the U.S.A. and at once came to visit Attilio in NYC, Attilio took Fermi to meet his colleagues at work, where Fermi and Kissinger very quietly recruited a sizeable portion of them for the super-secret "Manhattan Project."

[Attilio's page for cross-reference is directly accessible from
http://vilnajorgen.tripod.com/Attilio.html.]

Fermi's arrival suddenly pushed my father very high up on the popularity scale, but because my artist mother had been labeled a security risk for once selling a sculpture to the Moscow Art Museum and was now getting too many rave reviews from *The Socialist Worker*, the result was catastrophic.

The Secret Service investigation *very secretly* taking place prior to the hiring of my father who had been recommended by Fermi to join, and perhaps even eventually lead the medical team, intimidated all the art critics, who were either secretly gay or secretly socialist, and devastated my mother's career.

It also left Attilio behind, rejected from all medical promotions, without any explanation from Fermi.

(In a sinister way that was probably a favor, considering what was happening to the Rosenbergs! Was that why Fermi never even so much as dared contact us again?! Who framed them, I wonder? Who *really* gave the secrets to the Russians?) And we never would have known any of this were it not for my attendance at Hunter College where many of Attilio's colleagues, all grateful to Attilio, had retired to cushy new posts in the 1960's!

[Attilio's 1942 roommate - Michael Dacso, M.D., later 1966 Medical Dean of Albert Einstein Medical College - suddenly embraced me, a supposed total stranger applying for a medical writing job, planted a wet kiss on my cheek, and addressed me as *Annaselma*. Dacso's office was, strangely, inside the FBI building situated across the street from Hunter College. Dacso, a Hungarian, mysteriously retired and "vanished" a few weeks later, but not before leaving me two letters, preserved among my papers, documenting our meeting and his eagerness to see Attilio again.]

Suddenly both of my parents' careers, at first so promising, came to a halt, no reason given. Our scant savings were by then totally depleted. We had to move to a tenement and starve on minimal public assistance with only an occasional sale of Vilna's paintings to foreign collectors making a life-and-death difference.

Later, when Attilio finally got his medical license, out of desperation we moved to the suburbs to seek out an Italian ghetto desperately in need of a caring and affordable doctor.

We moved into Corona, Queens just before Christmas sometime around 1943 or '44, and we had no food. Then a small miracle happened - there was a knock on the door and the local undertaker brought us a basket of liquor (which, as I recall, we later traded for food). Behind him came the owner of the Italian delicatessen, *Signior* Bindo, a local big shot, with two baskets of deli delights. I never saw so much welcome junk food: meats, cheeses, and chicken in cans   with

ArtemisSmith's ODD GIRL *Revisited*

Henry VIII on the labels. (Rotisserie chickens were not in fashion in those days. Small pullets only came in large cans with oozing jellied gravy - but to us, then a delicacy!) Other neighbors followed, bringing homemade pies and cookies. (And the Bellaccico's also brought bread and kept on bringing bread for many years!)

Everyone was anxious to meet the new Italian-speaking family doctor. Despite the fact that we were Tuscans in the center of a Sicilian/Neapolitan divide, and that Attilio had to quickly learn all their dialects, it seems we had picked the right neighborhood after all! Well, at least, sort of.

Both of my parents were linguists fluent in more than eight languages. Having been born in Alexandria, Attilio spoke some Arabic as well as English, German, French, Italian, Spanish, Portuguese, Rumanian and Greek. So his practice quickly expanded from only impoverished distant relatives of notorious *Mafiosi* to every other ethnic group circling Corona: Irish, German, Greek, Armenian, and soon even the "black Muslims" of Flushing where he was the only physician who dared to make house calls - mostly on foot at first, for he didn't have a driver's license or a car. (Then we finally got an old Buick and the whole family accompanied Pappa on weekend house calls, in winter Helga and I shivering while huddled under blankets in the rumble seat.)

[Among the Flushing "coloreds" he was treated as a saint and became affectionately known as "de creepin' Jesus" because his knowledge of sickle cell anemia and other Mediterranean diseases worked slow but effective miracles on a group who could barely pay for any medical help at all. He also worked the same miracles on the Italian side of the tracks, but quietly.]

Had it not been for my father's unique skill as a diagnostician, his inter-ethnic/inter-racial medical practice would never have survived the neighborhood.

[On Junction Boulevard, a gaping hole in an empty lot where once a house had stood notoriously remained for years as a reminder to all "coloreds" never to cross the line into Corona.]

The dark-skinned Sicilians, Corsicans, Catanians, who had never been racists in the old country, were terrified of being identified and segregated as biracial and this caused the two communities, Muslim and Italian, to be openly at war. But our family was popular with everyone and as a ten-year-old I also played the violin and recited my poetry in many "colored" churches including the formerly segregated structure that still stands next to St. John the Divine.

One vivid childhood memory that deeply influenced my civil rights activism in later years happened when I listened in on a middle-of-the-night conversation between my father and mother. Usually they spoke in German so I wouldn't know what they were saying to each other. But this time it was either in Italian or English probably because they were so upset.

Attilio had returned from a house call to a prominent Italian family who begged him to sign a Caucasian death certificate for their 90-year old grandfather, once a negro slave, who had lived hidden in their attic for more than twenty years. The sun-starved pale old man had sat peering longingly from behind a shuttered window all those years while his progeny lived in fear lest they be exposed and bombed out of their home.

Of course Attilio signed it, and his good deed may have inadvertently caused us to be placed on a special protected families list kept by a super-secret biracial faction of the Mafia. From then on, no matter what neighborhood we walked in, it seems there were people seeing to it that we were kept safe (something that may have saved my life in the 1960's when the Hoover dirty tricks squad may have tried to spread the lie that I was an FBI informant).

Now everything got better.

The most powerful figure in the centuries-established Italian-American (i.e., Delano is also an Italian name) community into which our grandmother Ida and at least one of our great-grandfathers had been born, contacted and took personal note of us.

Dr. Armando Romano, Publisher of *Il Progresso,* invited us to dinner and brought us into the forefront by writing many reviews of Vilna's work and caused other Long Island newspapers to also take notice.

And Vilna, meanwhile, had the family join *The Sons of Norway* who eagerly welcomed all of us and especially our physician father. We became multinational again and wider and wider press notices followed.

Before then, what had been good for Attilio's practice had been devastating for the rest of us.

Vilna's paintings, once getting rave reviews

from Howard Devree and other critics at the *New York Times,* had gotten nowhere past 1943 and our education at the local grammar school, P.S. 16, left much to be desired - although I was able to form a special bond talking with my homeroom teacher, Miss Eckhardt, as I scrambled to keep pace with her and as she rushed to avoid me even while throwing out to me words of wisdom as we were walking home each day. (It never occurred to me until many *many* years later how strongly Billie Taulman resembled her in both appearance and manner. They were both Germanic school marms at heart!)

My passion for Miss Eckhardt's mental stimulus drove me to seek ever further afield. From the age of ten I knew how to travel alone to Manhattan, and it only cost a nickel. Taking my younger sister with me, for our intellectual survival we escaped Corona, then Elmhurst by subway at every opportunity, at first without, but soon later with, our parents' ready consent - once I showed them that it was really possible for us to 'legally' change schools.

Pretending that we were victims of a broken home staying with Ida who was now living with Valentina and Aldo and their son Augusto on Lexington Avenue, we cheated on the Board of Ed' and each and every school-day, and most weekends too, subwayed ourselves out of the ghetto.

[I went to Beha Junior High School which was the only all-girl school in Manhattan. My Arista class was filled with brilliant women some of whom later became famous, including a couple of call girls.]

Vilna meanwhile also learned from our example and pulled herself out of her depression, often took her paintings on the subway with us, and thereafter doggedly exhibited regularly in the Washington Square Outdoor Art Show with Attilio by her side whenever he could get away.

The Village crowd brought new contacts. Vilna soon managed to get the entire family as a unit invited to Uptown émigré chamber music salons that included one hosted by a "White Russian Princess and former Valkyrean operatic diva." The Princess was sponsoring a magnificent Russian cellist - comparable to Pablo Casals - who had gotten trapped on this side of the Iron Curtain while on a concert tour through South America: Maestro Bogumil Sykora, who became Vilna's and Helga's cello teacher. And he brought his new second family and distinguished South American patrons along to Queens. (His Russian family, already fully grown, remained in Russia, but he had a small baby with one of his students in the USA and, at a vigorous 75, was again a father.)

Now faculty and students from Julliard and Manhattan School of Music began to visit our own Friday-night musical soirees - at our new house in Elmhurst - and our circle of displaced persons grew to include many famous writers, artists and musicians anxious to trade private lessons for medical advice while clawing their way back up the ladder of success.

Again world-class celebrities were coming to *our* house, not yet exactly a palazzo but nevertheless *our* house no matter how humble and situated under the 'El where every time the trains went by the conversation had to pause!

[The Morpurgo Family is at least ten centuries old and has palazzos and castles in numerous locations in Europe. Our direct branch, situated in both Trieste and Venice, founded Generali A.G., whose Venetian corporate headquarters situated on the famous Piazza belonged to Giuseppe Lazzaro Morpurgo, undoubtedly a descendant of the proverbial Merchant of Venice. (As I told Lillian Hellman in the 1960's, when the Rothschilds were still peddling antiques on the streets of Paris, the Morpurgos were already wealthy bankers and financiers.)]

Toscanini's chosen successor at the Metropolitan Opera, Renato Cellini (one of the *Partigiani*), came often, as did his budding divas some of whom were my classmates at Forest Hills High School.

Dimitri Mitropoulos came once and touched our Chopin-vintage rectangular grand piano, probably only to buy it.

There were frequent performers who formed quartets and quintets for regular practice every Friday night: pianist-composer Julian White, oboist Harry Vas Dias, cellist Igor Horoshevsky, music teachers Cesare and Marjorie Borgia, the Kabay Ao siblings Gilopez and Marcellita who were debuting at Carnegie Hall. (All of these guys are on the internet - go Google them!)

My maestro, Edmund Zygman, Emeritus of the Philadelphia Philharmonic, usually conducted and brought his good friend, famed accompanist Arthur Balsam who consented to accompany and introduce *Philippino* Gilopez at Carnegie thereby guaranteeing full press coverage.

ArtemisSmith's ODD GIRL *Revisited*

And thanks to the Julliard students who were hoping to fix me up with him, I also got to meet my idol, child prodigy Ruggiero Ricci who was only a little older than I. But he was probably too shy to ask me on a date and we just shook hands and smiled at each other.

And that's how we survived our childhood!

[Do I resent any of it? No, I take Joy in having been displaced from the decadent life I would have been subjected to had we grown up in a Donna Reed neighborhood with a Donna Reed family. I am *very serious* when I say this: we Vikings know better; facing and overcoming the challenge of Adversity is the *only* road to Valhalla! Whatever doesn't kill you, etc., etc., ...]

Valentina, Aldo, Ida and Augusto, finally all on a ship to somewhere, c. 1942, joined us in NYC c. 1944.

ArtemisSmith's ODD GIRL *Revisited*

Dear Colleagues:

Have I rambled on too long? So what!

Too many footnotes? To blazes with that! They form a separate volume by themselves - read them later!

Go buy *"ArtemisSmith's* ODD GIRL Restored" (now also available as a E-Book) if all you really want is to read a classic pulp novel for your Gay Studies assignment! The beauty of a printed book is that you can always leaf through the pages, pick out what you want, and go back to the other parts later.

Disappointed in me? Deal with it! I've had it up to here with trying to get through to Ghetto-Gays! Grow up - look at the bigger picture - really come out of the closet and just be gender-free like me because times are changing again and you had better change with them!

For the rest of you, I promise I will not stop, I will continue, for this epistle has now become a hard-copy time capsule for some future cyborg, scanning through the zillions of information bits that may have scattered like shrapnel in today's information explosion

ArtemisSmith's ODD GIRL *Revisited*

Vilna Jorgen Morpurgo 1938 Rome, via Vasari
a student of Fokine, she danced with Nijinsky
at the Royal Ballet of Sweden

staged photo snapped from a lightbox camera
by daughter Annaselma, four years old

Vilna Jorgen 1938, photo staged by Vilna and snapped by four-year-old Annaselma. Vilna had studied with Fokine and danced with Nijinsky at the Royal Ballet of Sweden where Garbo was a classmate.

to catalog for a new species of *Munhood* to rediscover. It will resurface at a time when its relevance to a restyled culture seems more certain.

You may think I may have already told you a great deal about myself, perhaps too much, but in reality I have only scratched the surface.

A multitude of facts, and important persons, have been left out because I am not a journalist - or because there's way too much information for one book and you'll simply have to come back and buy more. Just call me GrandmaMoseX, finally ready to break her decades of silence. One reason I waited this long to write about my own life has been because I have a real problem both about preserving other people's secrets and about destroying the Rights Movements if I had said too much too soon. But *Hah!* now it's finally *my* turn - for I had to wait until many *many* persons had died so their lives would not be affected even by indirect insinuation. And even after they died, there remain things that, if I had been a priest receiving Confession, I would never *ever* allow myself to reveal.

That's why I have always turned to fiction as a means of telling the truth from a perspective that does not violate any particular person. Fiction deals with the generic rather than the particular - unless it's a "nonfiction novel" which I personally think is an atrocious fad, often doing extreme violence against the private person.

Capote, though he himself made good use of it, should never have left the genre for posterity to bastardize!

There is no such thing as "nonfiction."

All facts are corrupted by the observer.

Inter-subjectivity is the best we can hope for, and that too is shaky.

The whole purpose of seeking "Aesthetic Truth" is for us to scratch well below the surface, to seek out the universal in the particular.

Exploitation of any human being by the true artist is forbidden. An individual's right to privacy *always* needs to be respected. It doesn't matter whether that person may be living or dead, good or evil - their *name*, their *being*, and their *person* should be protected as Sacred - not because we need to believe in any god, but because we need to love and respect and approach *all* Humanity with humility.

It is with humility that I hope I am finally breaking my silence.

The only aesthetic rule I have been able to come up with for the necessary telling of my personal story - for not to tell it may do even more serious injury to Feminist and Gay and Arts histories as someday gathered up by cyborg search engines - is to reveal only those insights and events that will *do no harm* because not revealing them would do a greater harm and disservice to the very persons I cannot avoid including in this narrative.

I must be both artist and physician.

But communicating in real-time does not allow me enough breadth to encompass the full symphonic background of my thought. In my rush to inform, but not overload, I failed to provide sufficient context for the proper interpretation of many relevant early events and motivations. Let me now go back and close some of the gaps:

Let's go back to 1933 while I was still gestating in my mother's womb.

Vilna had been widowed for about three years but had never bothered to get a Parisian death certificate. To the world she was still married to Jorgensen; and especially to the Vatican - which required documentation of widowhood before allowing any new marriage certificate to be issued. Yet here she was, pregnant, and apparently by then very much in love, or so she said, to Attilio.

It would have been very easy, and not questioned by anyone, for her to say Jorgensen was my father, thereby bestowing upon me full 'Nordic-Aryan' genealogy. Why then marry an Italian Jew when, in Prague, Berlin, Paris and now in Rome as artist and journalist she had already been personally introduced to the "Nazi Elite" and knew exactly what kind of murdering scum were now at our door?

There she was, thirty-three and with her biological clock fast running out and still undecided whether or not it would be wiser to abort, still financially dependent upon commissions from Mussolini still rooming with von Blumenthal who painted her angrily as a new *Lola Montez* even while lecturing her in caustic German about how stupid and politically unrealistic Vilna's prospective marriage to Attilio would be.

ArtemisSmith's ODD GIRL *Revisited*

1965 Photo of Artemis Smith by Artemis Smith below the 1933 portrait of Vilna Jorgen painted by Weimar Post-Impressionist Clarissa von Blumenthal.

ArtemisSmith's ODD GIRL *Revisited*

Aldo and Vilna were already collaborating on architectural plans, still preserved among my papers, for a massive Arts Complex Mussolini had initially commissioned them to build. Vilna had already sculpted the building and grounds to be situated on a Roman hill and I remember seeing the model still intact at our apartment c. 1938. The project was dropped sometime after 1937 when Hitler told Mussolini to fire Aldo and Attilio and all other Italian Jews.

An important historical footnote was omitted from the First Edition of this Correlate and I might as well stick it in here coordinated with the opposite page:

[Mussolini, strong-armed mobster though he undoubtedly was, would never have willing allied himself with Hitler against the Allies on whose side he had fought in World War I. According to Vilna's eye-witness account, Italy did not capitulate willingly - it was invaded. Overnight, while the Black Shirts slept, the Brown Shirts took over. They entered Italy as an army of boys marching over the Alps in Loden gear. But then they grew, shot up almost overnight into beardless youths, their Brown Shirts unpacked, their ski cases opened to reveal smuggled rifles and bayonets. In Rome, an unarmed Civil Service was taken entirely unawares. The Swastikas were everywhere, and were everywhere in control.

(Does this sound like a *carte blanche* endorsement for contributing to the NRA? No, not really, but that's how it happened and how it well may happen again.)

By 1939, Attilio's colleagues, prudently wearing Black Shirts (which much later they traded for Partisan garb) saved our lives. In full Fascist uniform they raided the gallery where Vilna, by then furious with Mussolini's advances, by then having thrown away all concern for her own personal safety, was exhibiting a wall of Apocalyptic anti-Nazi art, hastily produced, the paint on the canvases not even dry.

Attilio's colleagues cut the canvases from their stretchers, rolling them up, "confiscating" them before they could be shown; they hushed up the press and "took us into protective custody" and in reality hastened all the paperwork that rushed us out of town.

[Perhaps some of those unsigned canvases have survived and

ArtemisSmith's ODD GIRL *Revisited*

Rome 1937 Gallery on Via Flaminia. What a pity a front view of this work is not shown for it was a masterpiece of Scandinavian Expressionism. The commission was to sculpt both Hitler and Mussolini, and each had one sitting with Vilna after which she blended their profiles into one warped and lifeless decapitated whole held aloft from the grave by a fallen people. After documenting that she had indeed fulfilled the commission, Vilna took a hammer and destroyed it, prudently declaring the work unfit to be shown. Meanwhile, we desperately hastened all of our preparations to get out of town.

may yet be found stashed away awaiting identification in some Vatican vault - though the paint was wet and, if not properly rolled, is probably all smeared which is why Vilna never even bothered to ask about what had been done with them when we visited Attilio's friends in 1963.]

Was von Blumenthal a lesbian?

Your guess is as good as mine. My feeling is that as a true artist she was simply post-gender.

Did Vilna have an affair with her?

Possibly but unlikely.

Scandinavian women are fiercely bisexual, preferring political lesbianism, sexual self-sufficiency to any subordination to the male sex. But not when admiring men are plentiful and Vilna was much in demand, not only by Aldo and Attillio but also all the single Scandinavian Consuls who were challenging Attilio to a drinking match to decide who was most fit to take her home until Vilna put a stop to it and dragged him out of the nightspot declaring wine-drinking Italians no match for vodka-drinking Vikings!.

Never did Attilio dare look at another woman in her presence. When dating Italians whose eyes wandered out of habit, Vilna would angrily use the back of their hands as an ashtray. That was the Scandinavian way and Attilio loved every bit of it. So did my uncle. So did every Italian she dated. As for the other nationalities she might have dined with - they all had better manners and did not need to be thus disciplined.

It may be quite possible that Aldo never had an affair with Vilna, since she was a chain smoker and he, like I, could not stand or go near avid smokers. Attilio, on the other hand, smoked a pipe defensively and didn't seem to mind. It is not uncommon for genes to cross between siblings, and that might be the only reason why I fortunately resemble Aldo, the prettier one, more than I do Roman-nosed Attilio. (Helga resembles Attilio but blonde hair and blue eyes makes all the difference!)

But as to the question of Vilna's possible political lesbianism, a long pause for a most memorable footnote to this must follow!

[When, during my "Anne Loves Beth" days I took a middle-aged friend suffering from a menopausal depression to Queens with me to stay overnight at my house so my father could provide her with extensive free medical attention, the following interesting conversation took place when I was alone with my mother: Said Vilna after a long silence, "D---- is a very nice girl." "Yes, Mother," I replied. After another pause, Vilna said: "A little masculine, though, don't you think?" "I suppose so," I shrugged. Again a pause. "She looks like a lesbian, doesn't she?" "Maybe" Again a pause. "Is she a lesbian?" "Yes, I think so," I said. "Do you know many lesbians?" "A few." "Have you been with a lesbian?" "Once or twice." And now a really long pause, after which, a sigh: "Well, as long as you don't make a habit of it!"]

It was not by Vilna's choice that she set me aside. Jorgensen's death certificate finally arrived from France only two days before I was born and my parents could finally be free to marry. The Fascists had been throwing red tape in the way and it finally had to be expedited by the Vatican which won a promise from Lutheran Vilna that she would baptize and raise me a Catholic, and by then Vilna had long ago decided to cast her lot with adoring Freemason Attilio for better or worse.

ArtemisSmith's ODD GIRL *Revisited*

For the first fifteen months of my infancy while working away at her canvases and sculptures my mother gave me all of her attention.

She took breaks and nursed me, spoke to me, played with me - I remember it all even though she spoke so many languages to me that I couldn't grasp a single word. So did both Aldo and Attilio play and hug and speak to me, and in so many languages that I couldn't grasp a single word they said either. Nor the words of my English and French-speaking grandmother!

My father's colleagues were giving me repeated nonverbal intelligence tests - the round pegs in the round holes variety - which I passed with record speed. Aldo was folding origami forms for me and I was imitating him. Fermi was testing my comprehension of mirror optics with delight.

But I was still without language.

Everyone was beginning to despair that there might be something wrong with me. Then, on a momentous occasion Ida reported that I finally uttered a very long and complicated sentence in what must have sounded much like Esperanto, and the mystery was solved.

From then on, everyone spoke only Italian to me and thanks to a tutor - an impoverished cousin on her way to Switzerland hired by Ida as part-time governess - I learned to read and write, add and subtract, before I was four. But I remained a parallel thinker, holding multiple hypotheses, working on everything at once like a media-blitzed geek. To this day there's still nothing linear about me.

As I have said, my song is a symphony. I despise

conversing in foreign languages, though I do read a few. I prefer instead to be a poet, and to use English well to make it the new *Lingua Franca* because not even the Chinese can agree on Chinese. (However, when I biked through Europe in 1962, I spoke Danny-Kaye-Dutch wherever I went and everyone understood me.)

So from 1936 on, no one can say my early childhood was deprived. I was the promising awaited-for new *Mozart* or *Leonardo* everyone fought over and laid claim to. (*But too bad she was born a girl,* everyone would add.) Even my aunt Valentina, herself a Chess Champion in Egypt, didn't give a damn whose child I was - as a Morpurgo genetic asset, to grow up with and breed more Morpurgo male prodigies, next to her own son I was also the star of the show.

My mother was the only one who had always really cared about me as a person, as an extension of herself, not as a genealogical *wunderkind*. But for a brief time in 1935, right after my sister Helga was born, there was a gap.

An inexplicable thing happened in the Tyrolean Alps where my father, drafted into military service, had quarantined himself inside a fascist youth camp to prevent a general outbreak of diphtheria.

There were no cell phones in those days. It took time to send a message either by radio or whatever.

Vilna had been left stranded on a mountain top with only me and my seriously ill infant sister and no servants to assist her. We were in a small cabin surrounded by a precipitous drop on three sides. When playing outside, I had to be harnessed on a long chain like a dog for my own safety.

ArtemisSmith's ODD GIRL *Revisited*

(My only memory of that period is of reaching out but not grabbing the udders of a goat as a tinkling Alpine herd went by. Or maybe I also do remember someone finally giving me some milk and berries).

Vilna was also very ill, or maybe she had just given birth unattended. She had always had pernicious anemia and anorexia but she was also suffering from heavy metal poisoning - lead, cadmium, chromium - from all the paints in her palette. When she worked she would forget to eat and slip ever more deeply into a creative trance and, being hungry, would begin sucking absently on her paint brushes because the metals tasted sweet.

Not a very good thing for a lactating mom!

Not a good thing at any time! (Attilio didn't notice until the telltale black lines of lead poisoning showed on Vilna's gums - but that was later. There was a chelating treatment for that, but not for the anemia. It had gone on too long. There was progressive nerve damage, not all of it reversible.)

On top of that mountain Vilna suffered some kind of lapse of mind - not because she was insane, just poisoned and chronically malnourished.

Like Van Gogh possibly, but fortunately not quite as bad.

Something happened that early spring or summer in the Alps in 1935 and Vilna couldn't explain it but throughout her life she would go back to trying to explain herself, to apologize to me. She repeatedly related the event to me as follows:

ArtemisSmith's ODD GIRL *Revisited*

> "I can't believe what a good child you were even though I had to tie you to the house to keep you from falling down the mountain. You played quietly by yourself and found things to do and never cried. And I feel so guilty for neglecting you - I did not want to neglect you - your sister was just so sick and I was just so exhausted and anemic, and had no servants to help me, and I don't even know how I managed to save Helga's life since she was allergic to my milk and I couldn't breast feed her. I can't remember more than that except that I somehow made a puree of beef and vegetables for her and she eventually got better."

[The story is bizarre and lends itself to another interpretation, offered - then finally rejected - by Lillian Hellman in the 1960's, when she first sought me out, then my sister Helga, still in search of Julia's child, the lost Rothschild heiress. Did my infant sister die and did Vilna go into post partum? Did someone sneak another baby in the crib? Possible but not credible - Helga strongly resembles both sides of the family.]

Every time my mother recited her guilty confession through the years I tried to tell her that she had never neglected me - that she was the best mother I could possibly have had. That I completely understood all the suffering she had undergone. But when she tried to hug me I could scarcely ever allow it. Her emotional need for me was too great, and it would have destroyed me. And her mind, her insights, though unique and astounding, would sometimes twist and become temporarily impossible to reason with. But given time to reflect on it, reason would finally prevail to a degree often matching or surpassing Attilio.

[After that, I never met Helga until I was put into the same baby carriage with her and returned to my parents' apartment on Via Vasari. She was then more than a merely healthy infant, but still a cry baby. Her facial features are those of Attilio, and all our cousins agree that she looks like their cousins and is definitely a Morpurgo child despite Hellman's suspicions to the contrary. Helga doesn't want me to write about her so I will keep my notes to a minimum. But some things need to be said: Helga grew up blaming Vilna for all of her problems and those of Attilio, but that was totally misguided. Instead of opposing Vilna's confusions, Helga always humored her and that caused Vilna to lose her way. I always fought with Vilna and told her exactly when and how she was doing something wrong - especially in her art work. She loved me for it, depended on me for it. When I left to live on my own, Vilna obsessed over my absence and Helga resented that and blamed me for abandoning her to Vilna. She has always felt closer to Attilio.]

It's so complicated.

Vilna was my first love, and as my mother she had a right to be. But we had problems.

I remember that when she finally reclaimed me, she took me back in bed to nap with her to try to make up for all the hugging I had missed in the year or two she couldn't be with me, and of course I reacted as any small child would and sought her breast, whereupon she, in sudden shock and fear pushed me away saying "No, you are too old for that now and it was because I breast fed you that I am now losing my teeth." Whereupon, devastated but comprehending, I took the rejection as final and kept my distance.

There could never be a going back.

Throughout my life I wanted desperately to hug my mother - but there were also other gut reasons why I couldn't approach her.

At the risk of sounding evasive or wacky, to hell with blaming it all on the Nazis and Fascists - as a small child affected only by the intense fear generated in that period, I distanced myself from the stench of fear like a small dog trying to find a corner of the room where I could turn my nose to the wall.

Dirty Jews they called us. With good reason. We stank. And the stench of chain-smoking Jews was the worst. Not only chain-smoking Jews but my non-Jewish mother too. The horrible mix of tobacco-saturated fear constantly assailed my supersensitive nostrils.

A chemical reaction, not a psychological one.

So there you have it - put the blame for all of my family's dysfunctions squarely where it lies - on the tobacco industry; for as all of the grownup events were unfolding, I remember spending my entire childhood distancing myself from my parents, gasping for clean air.

Not only then but later.

Elusive as it sounds, their chain-smoking was the whole reason for my running away from my parents as soon as I could get away. I couldn't live with the stench and the smog, and when my parents finally listened and quit the foul habit in the 1960's, I was finally able to spend more time with them.

Dear Colleagues:

1949.

[When Ida, Aldo and Valentina moved to an upper-class Jewish neighborhood, we enrolled in Forest Hills High School where nearly all of my Depression-era teachers had doctorates and many of my classmates went on to fame and fortune. It was grad-school-level education.]

At fifteen and now living in Elmhurst as a Forest Hills High School sophomore, I had won an acting scholarship to the famed *Midtown Drama Center* directed by Natalie Donnet where George Bartenieff was a classmate and his mother, Irmgarde Bartenieff, was my dance teacher. (I dated George's older brother Igor once but that went nowhere because he smoked.)

I used that backdrop for my opening scene in "Anne Loves Beth" but I swear to you that I never *ever* had a crush on Natalie who was smoking and eight months pregnant at the time! My mind by then was on many *many* other things.

ArtemisSmith's ODD GIRL *Revisited*

"The Family Quartet" c. 1949. At our own house in Elmhurst. Vilna and Attilio were the only serious music students.

ArtemisSmith's ODD GIRL *Revisited*

With Vilna, Attilio, Aldo and Fermi as my role models, my scientific, artistic, literary and acting careers were all taking off simultaneously and the time for childhood crushes on either mother or father figures had already long passed. (I was initially preparing to become a medical doctor or a physicist or a mathematician, but at post-puberty I finally chose the arts. I think my hormones had a lot to do with that.)

Distinctly with career in mind I connected with two vastly different new mentors: Sidney E. Porcelain of the Jeanne Hale Literary Agency and John Burgess Hillsbury, my acting coach.

Neither was the first to shape me, for I had already gone through quite a few mentors and maestros prior to them and found others after them, but they were the right coaches for that time in my life.

[My first literary mentor, and first crush, David Gillerlean, was a tall, dark-Irish English teacher who spent his entire summer vacation procrastinating on his own try for a Pulitzer by teaching me gratis how to analyze poetry and prose while his wife and daughter tolerated my precocious pre-teen intrusion. If he had not been already married, I would have run away with him in a heartbeat!]

Burgess was unbending, an exacting task master; in a few short weeks he totally transformed me from a chubby unkempt tomboy first to a *Miss Piggy* and later to a full-blown *Barbie*, dressing me up like the Ziegfeld dolls he made for a living on the side which are now worth a small fortune.

Burgess put himself and me on a diet, coached me to walk and talk like an ivy league debutante and stylized me for Shakespeare, Broadway and teen photo shoots. He got me to trade my sneakers for spiked heels, to die my long auburn hair a blazing topaz and to pound the pavement on rounds for both of us to all the talent agencies.

[I did not realize myself what kind of swan I had become. No longer always in the shadow of Helga's blonde and blue-eyed accompaniment, I now found myself surrounded by a crowd of suitors, mostly from N.Y.U., who later became architects, engineers, famous journalists - and none of whom could tempt me - even by dangling marriage - to give up my virginity before I turned eighteen.]

Together we auditioned howbeit in vain to the Actors' Studio and just about everywhere else as my own list of theatrical contacts grew. Burgess was a perfect Henry VIII to my Anne Boleyn. His hairline now receding, he might once have passed for Elvis or a young Orson Welles.

But he smoked like Vilna.

Porcelain was a nonsmoker, and I really preferred writing to acting so he became my most frequent side-kick.

Handsomer than either Bob Hope or Phil Silvers, Porcelain was cut out of the same cloth, many-talented, always ready with a joke. He had run away from home while in his early teens to join the Army at the beginning of World War II, where he was given an I.Q. test and was immediately pulled out of the ranks and shoved into Officers' Training School then into Military Intelligence - even while he continued to entertain his fellow troops with his singing, piano playing and composing.

ArtemisSmith's ODD GIRL *Revisited*

After the war, he got a scholarship to Columbia, all the way to a Masters' in English with a minor in Communications and ended up teaching English there as an adjunct, if I remember correctly.

Porcelain and I were so much alike that when we first met I at once decided I would marry him. But he was twenty years older and I quickly reconsidered. Still, we told everyone we were engaged - so they would stop thinking we were secretly having an affair.

The mock engagement kept me from becoming "compromised" in my anxious father's eyes, whose position in the moralistic Italian community was growing sensitive now that I was fast-becoming such an artistic Lolita. It also kept all of Porcelain's transient house guests, usually sex-hungry prison parolees angling to become the next Spillane, away from me.

Porcelain encouraged me to submit my plays for professional readings at Ray Yates' *Dramatists' Forum* and there I met many professionals and started my own drama workshop; at sixteen and about to graduate high school, I became an overnight regular on Washington Square, the youngest member and favorite protégé of the *Forum,* directing the reading of my plays while also appearing in the Chorus at the original Amato Opera on Bleecker and at the Gilbert and Sullivan Provincetown Players on McDougal.

[A couple of years later in my professional spare time as an advertising executive, out of sheer love and respect for the artistry of Judith Malina and Julian Beck I also swept floors, collected contributions and eventually did bit parts for *The Living Theater* in a play by Paul Goodman where just about every fourth word was a four-letter word. But alas, not while they were still at the Cherry Lane where they had done Stein, Jarry and Picasso..]

Porcelain, like most highly creative persons I have known, had a racy sense of humor. Though he never used four-letter words his outlandish puns often shocked the eavesdroppers in the crowd.   Nothing and no one was safe from his wit. I wonder how Anita Hill would have reacted to him rather than to Clarence Thomas! In the 1950's it was very cool to talk dirty.

With that kind of open attitude, it was easy to make Porcelain my sounding board for all the works I did not want to immediately show my parents, including "Anne Loves Beth."

[Porcelain   seemed to know just about everything about just about everyone. It was even rumored that he had been part of the formative CIA If so, then he was definitely more like a superhero acting as double-agent, always on the side of Truth, Justice and the *Real* American Way. Most of his life he lived in frugal, nearly abject poverty. When I first met him, before he moved to a brownstone studio off Union Square, he was sleeping in a Midtown closet-sized office that you could barely crawl into because it was stuffed with manuscripts, sheet music and a piano - and there was no floor space - to play the piano he had to sit on the bed. No! Get your mind out of the gutter.   Porcelain was never my lover - from the first to the last he was never more than like a father to me.!]

ArtemisSmith's ODD GIRL *Revisited*

Dear Colleagues:

I have a confession to make: "Anne Loves Beth" now available in a separate pocket edition, as well as in E-Books, was not my first novel. Nor was it my first offering as a budding cultural revolutionary and master-builder. Bear with me - you really do want to know what a fifteen-year-old virgin high school student does with her spare time after she gets through with her homework:

It must have been around 1950 when McCarthyism began and a number of my teachers - some of the nicest ones - were suddenly fired as former Communists/communists or whatever, mostly for being New Dealers or open members, advocates or defenders of the Socialist Workers' Party.

At Forest Hills the infamous Loyalty Oath had become a prerequisite for a high school diploma, and many Jewish students, sensitive to its future implications, refused to sign it.

ArtemisSmith's ODD GIRL *Revisited*

A Loyalty Oath was also a prerequisite for remaining a naturalized citizen and I had no problem with loving the U.S.A. and saluting the American Flag and defending the U.S. Constitution. But obviously McCarthyism was decidedly un-American. That presented me with a dilemma for it personally would have required a greater sacrifice on my part to defend Truth, Justice, and the *Real* American Way than anyone born here.

Though inwardly a super hero, I dared not get involved. I stood apart, prudently silent.

But I nevertheless felt I needed to take some kind of stand with my classmates, to speak out against the system in some form that would also get *me*, an honor student, into serious trouble - perhaps even expelled.

I found my own way.

Witness my first political manifesto, secretly preserved all these years thanks to Vilna. I just found it tucked away neatly when finally going through her papers.

My apologies for all the misspellings. This is only the original first draft - edited before distributed.

[This was also my high school payback for an earlier experience in grammar school when, upon being prompted by my classmates to draw anatomically correct pictures of Adam and Eve, I was ratted on and forced to apologize to the entire class for prematurely contributing to their sex education.]

I produced the work on my portable typewriter, printed on yellow pulp layered with about eight carbons. I typed it about three times, ending up with a limited edition of about 27 copies, redrawing the cartoons freehand for each batch. Then I folded and stapled each pamphlet and delivered it personally to each of my teachers.

Alas, the work was immensely well-received.

The Assistant Principal, Rene Fulton, who deserves to be commended and immortalized for her wit and perception, called me into her office and instead of expelling me, offered me a full scholarship to Bennington!

Fulton was a statuesque brilliant older woman who looked a lot like movie star Alexis Smith and I wanted so much to say *yes, yes* to her, *yes* to an ivy league girls' school - but a panic suddenly took hold of me.

I blurted out that I did not want to go to any women's college because I had already been to an all-girl junior high school and I did not want to grow up a lesbian!

In my heart, however, I suddenly realized precisely why I was afraid. And again, in my own way, I decided to face down my fear.

Next came "Anne Loves Beth."

Here then, reprinted for posterity is what my teenage *angst* should reveal about me.

Pause now, and *Enjoy!*

[If you are reading an abridged E-Book Edition that does not include this, you will find it available for free online reading at http://larsennilsenvinje.tripod.com/Pro1.html in my preliminary web-interactive sketch pad for this volume.]

ArtemisSmith's ODD GIRL *Revisited*

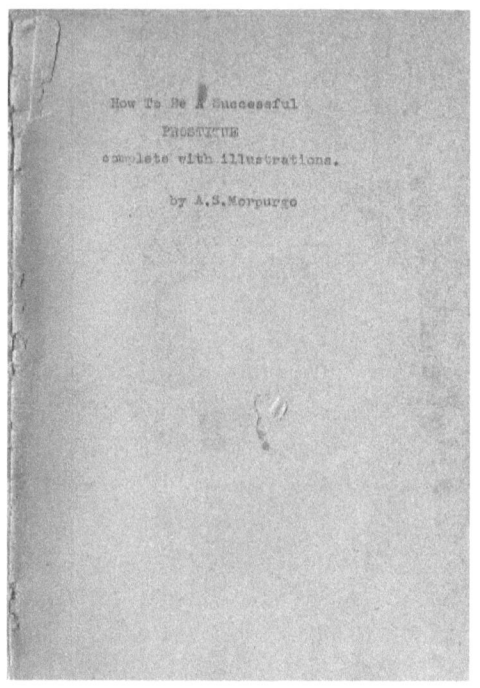

"How To Be A Successful Prostitute (complete with illustrations)"
© 1950 by A.S. Morpurgo. All rights reserved.

To
The Faculty of Forest Hills High School
upon their adoption of
McCarthyism

This is strictly a work of fiction based upon the Author's investigative infiltration of the 1949 Greenwich Village Arts Scene. No resemblance to actual places or persons living or dead is intended.

ArtemisSmith's ODD GIRL *Revisited*

I have been prostituting myself for years
and no one has yet raised an eyebrow.
Here's hoping someone will.

ArtemisSmith's ODD GIRL Revisited

MAMMA

was a whore the day I was born.

I sold my smiles for the great price of
food, love, and shelter. Even at that early
age I sat on gentlemen's laps. One particular
customer would always repay me with a candy
drop, but I'd have to work awfully hard for
it.

He had a long beard which always made me
sneeze, and I always knew what he'd eaten
for lunch.

Pappa was my favorite.

He helped me undress and get into bed.

But it wasn't until I started school that
I received a real challenge to my talents.

Teacher was an old maid but I always called
her Mrs. I got an A on my report card.

ArtemisSmith's ODD GIRL Revisited

My first crush was on a little boy with glasses. I thought he was the philosophical type.

I admired him from a distance but my charms had no effect. He was too tall for me.

When I was seven I decided to become a
gypsie. I sang to the people in the
streets and they gave me nickels to stop.
I decided I wasn't making enough money for
my talents and so I took up a new approach.

[Drawing of a child holding a cup and a sign reading "I WANT TO BE A MILLIONAIRE PLEASE CONTRIBUTE"]

I painted a sign and sat on the corner with
a little cup. From then on I never needed
an allowance.

ArtemisSmith's ODD GIRL *Revisited*

By the time I entered high school, my
talents became more subtle; possibly because
I had to wear considerably more underwear.

I went in for high heels with bobby-socks
and dungarees with long hanging earrings.
However I never did learn how to smoke.
I decided I was warm enough.

I became an anti-moralist and was enrolled
into the Satan, Witches, and Devil-worshippers'
Secret Society in school. To be eligible
for membership I had to be iniciated.

The other girls had it in for me and thought
they would really make it tough. I had to
go around saying "I've gotta go." to
everyone who spoke to me for five days.
I had a lot of fun.

After my second year I began to take things seriously and operated on a strict business basis. I used to rent out my old boy friends to my less fortunate colleagues. It was then that I started a friendship club.

It went along fine until the teachers wanted to join.

I decided to use my talents in more
specialized fields. I took up writing,
acting, directing, art, music, and dance.
I also dabbled in philosophy, anthropology,
(the
      study of man), Freudian psychology,
and biology. It wasn't long before I became
a walking encyclopedia.

But even there I was forced into prostitution.
It seemed that the only way to tell the truth
was to lie. Especially when all-knowing teachers
were wrongly insisting they were right. Oh
well, the poor souls were happy in their
misery.

During my intellectual period I took up the violin. My teacher was a handsome Italian with a French accent.

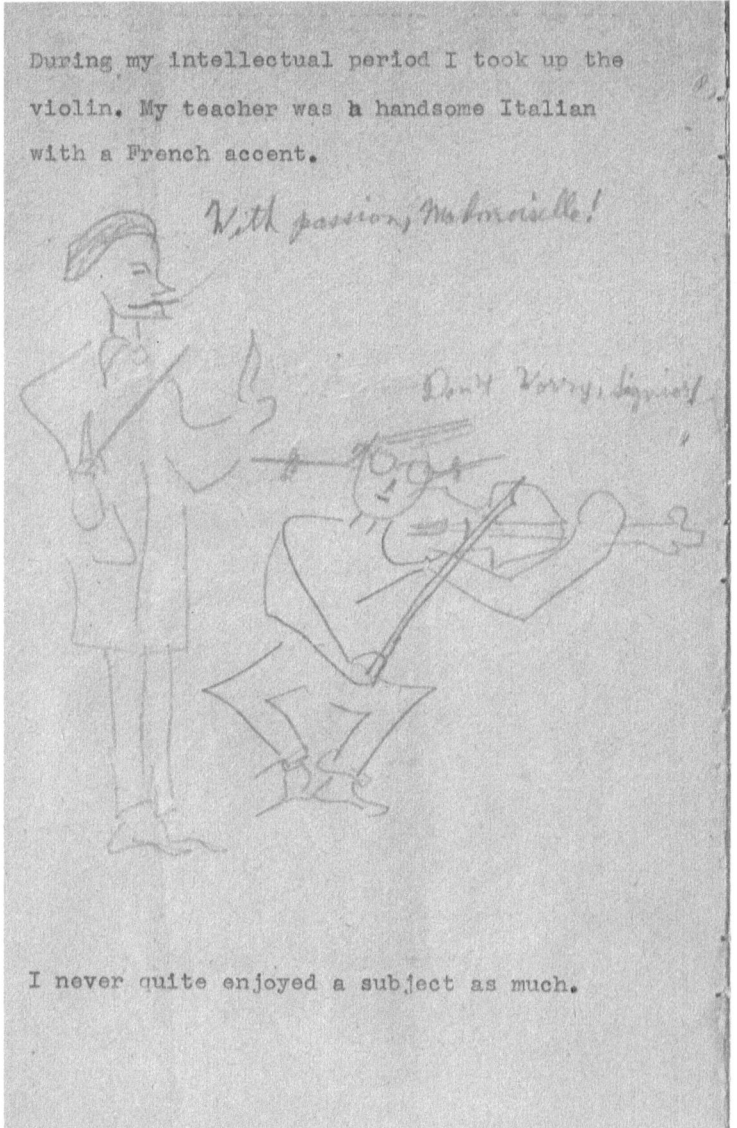

I never quite enjoyed a subject as much.

By the time I graduated from school I had grown tired of mem. I became an actress and married the theater.

I decided to start working in Burlesque. I was so talented I was banned.

ArtemisSmith's ODD GIRL *Revisited*

I finally gave up acting and became a writer. This period of my life I call "My Intellectual Lean Years." This was due to the fact that I was determined to give up prostitution in all forms, and refused to right commercially. All my friends praised my scripts without even bothering to read them. I considered it a great tribute.

At the height of my career I was forced to stop. I had developed hemmoroids from

Love re-entered my life in the form of a
blonde interne I met while recovering in
the hospital. I insisted that he change
all my bandages. Two weeks later he proposed.

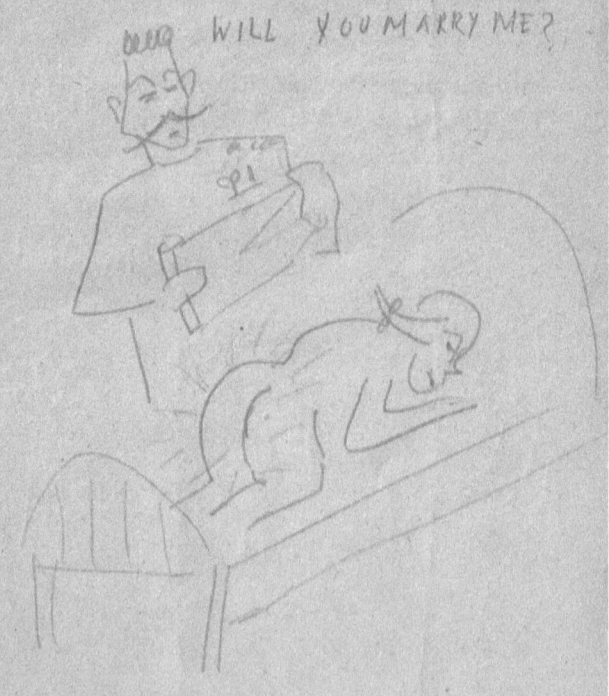

After considerable thought I said no! I
wanted to remain a free woman.

My parents finally decided it was about time
I got a job. They wouldn't support me
anymore. I began to write commercially.
Rejection slips poured in and the garbage
man began to resent my existence.

The postman and I became good friends. It
wasn't until a year later that I learned
he had a wife. Oh well----.

Seeing that I was getting nowhere I decided
to find an agent. I found several and they
all wanted to teach me how to write, for a
small fee, of course.

you're beautiful!

that's a weak adjective

I chose one and wound up teaching him.

My parents were putting the pressure on me again so I decided to take a part time job in an orchestra. But it seemed that I had payed more attention to my teacher's accent than to what he was saying, and so I was not such a good musician. However, the conductor seemed to think I added something to the orchestra anyway, so he wrote in a special part for me. I think I was in the only orchestra in New York City that hired a fourth violinist.

I warned him that I could only play first, second, and third violin but I did not know how to play fourth. He said it didn't make any difference. I could use a standard violin.

That year I made money.

ArtemisSmith's ODD GIRL *Revisited*

With my steady income and peace of mind I
found it hard to get inspiration. I decided
to frequent Cafe society. I met some very
interesting characters, and I began a new
policy of writing from experience.

This new policy had its bad points since most
of the things I experienced were unprintable.

By this time I had decided that the best thing for me to do was marry a millionaire. Equipped with silk stockings and high heels I set out hunting.

I met a few but they were already married.

Finding life intolerable at home, I got myself an appartment. Due to the housing shortage I could only find one in most unpleasant surroundings. The landlady was a fat old whore who kept a sign in all her rooms. "No Gentlemen Or Dogs Allowed." Despite these hard restrictions I was forced to take it.

One night a friend came to visit me and brought another friend along; a man. Heavens! The landlady eyed them suspiciously as they climbed the stairs but didn't say anything. Two hours passed and nothing happened. Then there was a knock on the door. I answered, and sure enough it was old fat-face.

"I've come up, " she said solemnly as I sought an explanation, "to bring these extra pillows."

I was overjoyed to find out that her rule did not apply to all men, only to gentlemen.

ArtemisSmith's ODD GIRL Revisited

A rich uncle died and left me a fortune. I thought that at last I'd have no need to sell myself anymore. How wrong I was. My inheritance taxes were so high that I had to go to work to pay them. However, the tax collector was such a nice fellow that he showed me how to deduct here and there until I broke even. But some good did come out of my inheritance. Before I could even inherit paying the inheritance taxes I had to get a college education which was provided for me. And so off I went.

In order to further my education on the subject I was most interested in, I decided to take a general Bachelor's Degree. I always thought they were fascinating people.

ArtemisSmith's ODD GIRL *Revisited*

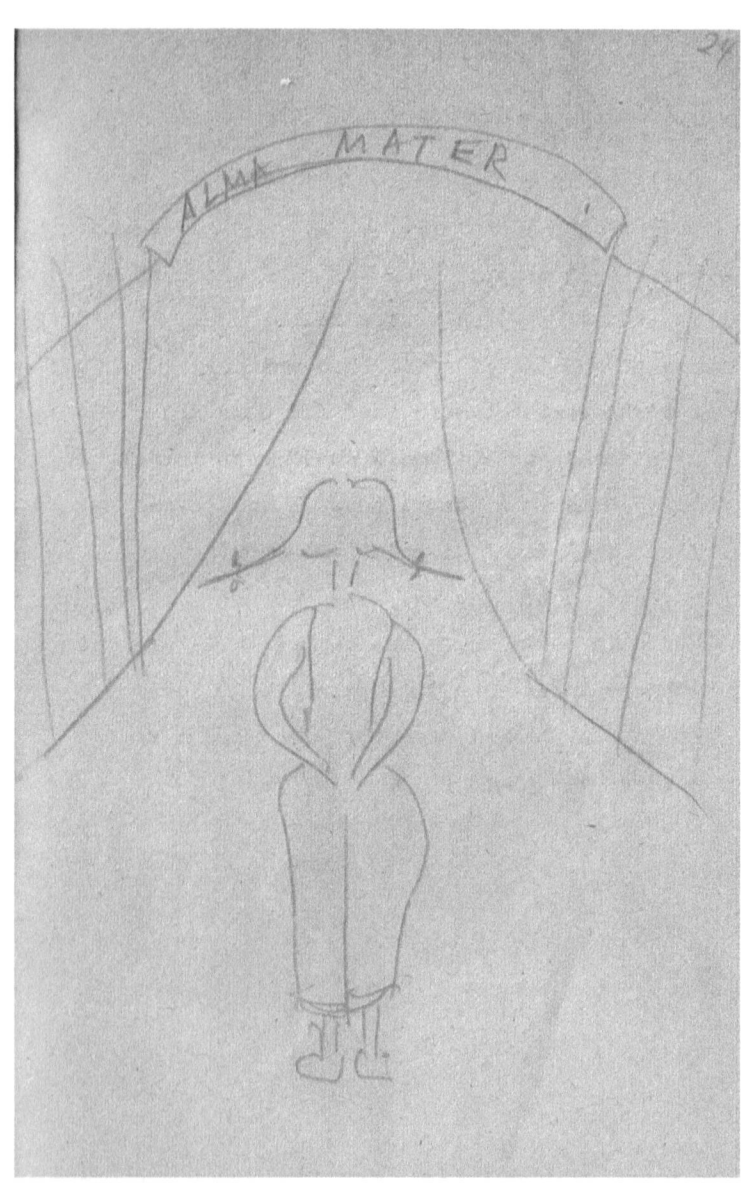

My roommate was a benzedrine fiend. We had a wonderful time staying up together and

exchanging advice on what do do about dried-up boyfriends.

As in all colleges this one also had sororities. But they were all so snooty that I decided to start my own and allow boys in. After considerable opposition I finally founded the Grasshoppers, Ants and Worm Eaters' Society for the Prevention of cruelty to beef. The cows thanked us, but there are rumors that among the insects a reward has been offered for my carcass,

They don't taste good!

ahah, a caterpillar!

dead or alive. At least, I can't have a picnic on the grass without being bitten by some ferocious police bug.

ArtemisSmith's ODD GIRL *Revisited*

I became interested in journalism and wrote in the Campus Gazzette. The newspaper went out of print within two issues. It seems my editorials were a bit too heated for the faculty to allow it to continue.

> The Three F's
> 1. Free Speech
> 2. Free Press
> 3. Free Love

After a long hard battle they finally consented to put it back in press, providing

ArtemisSmith's ODD GIRL *Revisited*

By the end of my first year at college
a campaign had been started to have me expelled.
It seems that the parents thought I was
corrupting the morals of their precious brats.
I merely laughed and told them to go ahead
and try.

I was determined to learn my trade even
thought there were no classes on the subject.

During my college years my youth bloomed to its fullest and I stopped wearing dungarees.

May I carry your books?

It got so bad that I couldn't even walk across

I decided to put a stop to it, so I cut my hair up short and wore men's clothes. The result was disastrous.

The men stopped looking and the girls started.

After some thought I concluded that I should be proud to look sexy, so I wore transparent dresses. The campus was one of the most picturesque in the world.

y benzedrine roommate introduced me to
a handsome young alcoholic who invited me
to go out on a binge with him.

accepted

My happy college life was ended with the arrival of my diploma. I had learned all about Bachelors and came in first of my class. My society gave me a little present to remember them by. The inscription read---To our venerable, most beloved founder, who's pioneering has opened the way for other to follow in her footsteps.

With tears in my eyes I thanked them all, feeling that finally I had become successful in my proffession. Slowly, in transparent dress and cap and diploma, I walked away from my Alma Mater.

Now I was all set.

ArtemisSmith 1949

ArtemisSmith's ODD GIRL *Revisited*

Dear Colleagues:

"Class of 1951."

Thank you, Rene Fulton! I graduated high school with honors and a full Regents scholarship but I didn't feel the need for college. Forest Hills had the highest academic rating in New York State thanks to all the Ph. D's on their faculty that they were now firing.

I had already been to college, and grad school too. I was ready for my life now. The only thing I felt the need for was fresh air, to be able to breathe fresh air as quickly as possible, to get away from the stench of tobacco at my house which my sister didn't seem to mind at all.

[Helga apparently never forgave me for not taking her with me. She wanted to move into Manhattan too. She had always clung to me since infancy and could never understand why I didn't feel as close to her as she to me. But our minds and abilities were totally different. I had always found it impossible to work with her - we would never see eye-to-eye and would always end up quarreling. We had little in common. Besides, she was a blonde - what romantic chance would I have had with her tagging along?}

ArtemisSmith's ODD GIRL *Revisited*

My mother and I were constantly at odds - not because we didn't love each other but because we loved each other too much. Vilna saw me as her clone, and I also saw me as her clone, and *I* certainly couldn't survive being that creatively close to her. I had to break out on my own.

I firmly announced to both parents that it was now time for me to move out of the house and live by myself. There was no future for me in *any* Queens ghetto, and my career was already on its way. My two mentors were also making it easy for me. Burgess was moving in with retired Chicago theater critic Robert Garland (of William Randolph Hearst and *Citizen Kane* fame. I had frequent talks with Garland but got little information on anything important) and had given me his low-rent 10 x 18 professional hole-in-the-wall on Park Avenue South which was coming down in a year or two but so what; *plus* there was an opening, and Porcelain had recommended me, as an assistant at the Jeanne Hale Literary Agency - my first paying job.

Enough said! *Basta! Finito!*

Vilna, though she desperately wanted me at home, unselfishly approved. (This was exactly what Vilna had done at sixteen. And my graphic novel matched her first satirical journal, all about her Left Bank life in Paris, published by the Scandinavian press.)

Attilio hesitantly consented.

I moved out, "engaged," emancipated, and all set to do exactly as I pleased and decided, like my graphic protagonist, that I would not become a lesbian - at least not right away. Instead I would start dutifully dating men more seriously (nonsmoking men) and see where that took me. It would be more than another year before I decided to indulge my curiosity and investigate women, (nonsmoking women) and of course had to write about it.

Despite its precarious marketability, both Porcelain and Jeanne Hale were encouraging me to finish "Anne Loves Beth" as a valid work that would eventually find a publisher.

Hale, who owned *Golden* Books and half of E.M. Hale and Company - the Midwest classroom textbook giant - was pushing the system toward early sex education in the schools and even had the hope that in fifty years or so my book might become a classroom standard.

[Jean Karl, immediately later head of American Library Association, was one of the first persons to review the pulp version when it came out circa 1957. She was kind enough to make dinner for me and Taulman - *twice*, since to my deep chagrin I had forgotten all about her first invitation. Karl was instrumental in seeing to it that *Odd Girl* was gradually put on public library bookshelves nationwide. Thank you, Jean Karl, most courageous Librarian!]

"Anne Loves Beth" filled a special need: no guidebook existed to assist the young in avoiding the hurdles of an illicit society almost wholly dependent upon an organized-crime network for its existence.

Written by a teenager, for other teens, it had the potential to be such a guidebook for the deviant young, to help them navigate away from deranged predators and toward some measure of normalcy - to be presented from a viewpoint that spoke directly to the sexually confused in a manner they could relate to and accept.

But the market wasn't ready for it in 1953 and by 1957 time was growing short - the civil rights movements were starting and someone else was bound to come out with a similar work before me. I had the opportunity to sell it to Beacon Books. It would not be in hard cover but it might get noticed anyway. It was a desperate but essential move.

Hale agreed but Porcelain didn't, so I switched agents from Porcelain to Hale and rushed to publish in the yellow sheets even as I continued to revise and polish the work which represented my adolescent tour of the 1950-52 NYC bar scene while I was concurrently studying, writing, acting and directing - and dating mostly nonsmoking men, in those days an endangered species!

[My poetry, other novels and plays, including *Hark the Pterodactyl, The Peacock Has Ugly Feet, Brother Thanatos,* and *Testament of Sarah,* being worked on simultaneously, were of the existentialist genre reinforced by my 1962 trip to Europe where, thanks to Isadora's brother Raymond Duncan, I gained a most precious interview with Alice Toklas that left me blessed with an immortal wound. *Ask me about that on a talk show!*]

Turning to the pulps was again an act of rebellion.

I didn't give a damn if the theme and its racy presentation would tweak the noses of the ultra-conservative publishing establishment.

Hale, herself a cultural revolutionary, agreed.

ArtemisSmith's ODD GIRL *Revisited*

It is foolish to believe that pulp fiction can be kept out of the hands of minors. I got my first glimpse of the genre at eleven, browsing in the back of my local candy store. It was the confusion generated by such false portrayals of sexual reality that prompted my adolescent resolve not to disinform. (But it was there that I also later purchased my first issue of *One Magazine* and through it happily connected to One, Inc. and Mattachine.)

Despite the fact that Beacon Books (Universal Publishing and Distributing Corp.), was a publisher of last resort, and that the book that was finally published was not the final author-approved version, I still maintain that I made the right choice not to wait.

But now let my own version be on record: "Anne Loves Beth" is the restored and proper fictionalized NYC tourist guide as it was originally intended by me. I make no apology for its radical viewpoint. I meant it to strike a literary death blow to the system not because I identified myself as "Gay" but because at that time feminism was tied to political lesbianism.

The entire system was rotten, everything had to change - all at once - come what may!

By then I was partnered with Billie Ann Taulman and no longer Hale's assistant. Still not having a college degree but always passing as post-graduate, the two of us had elbowed our way into Advertising and Public Relations while attending evening sessions together as undergrads at Hunter College.

Activism came naturally as part of the job.

ArtemisSmith's ODD GIRL *Revisited*

Since 1954 I had taken a founding role in most of the human rights movements, including early underground racial integrationist organizations which later merged into C.O.R.E. (Committee On Racial Equality).

J. Edgar Hooverism and *Joe McCarthyism* were still rampant, and what later became known as "the rainbow coalition" was then fomenting in widely different circles and multiple private gatherings at the homes of well-heeled members of loosely organized semi-secret liberal factions opposing the tyranny of H.U.A.C.

Being professionally well-connected, I, Porcelain, my ex-husband Jerry (Gerald Rauch, former Columbia Pictures Manager for the Caribbean, ousted and diplomatically hustled on a plane back to the USA c. 1952 for his anti-Trujillo activities in the Dominican Republic; our marriage did not last although we remained friends and I eventually got an annulment) and Taulman, grouped together and moved freely among such activist-literary-artistic circles sometimes later (c. 1957) also attended by Hale, who was a drinking pal of Maimie Eisenhower and had just been appointed a human rights advisor to Ike. (Though also a work of fiction, my third pulp novel, *This Bed We Made,* originally titled "For Immediate Demolition", captures the atmosphere of that stage in my life which was filled with many more persons and events than I can take time to relate to you here but will probably fill in elsewhere.)

[Though at heart a liberal, key staunch Republican Hale was also on a first-name basis with Richard Nixon, Joe McCarthy, Roy Cohn and J. Edgar

Hoover, as well as Nancy Davis Reagan, to whom Hale introduced me and my poetry and plays c.1965. The continuity from the Eisenhowers to the Nixons to the Reagans with respect to their role in all the civil rights movements may have centered around Hale and her closest friends and may have had far more strategic import than has yet been revealed. In 1965 Hale and Mrs. Reagan graciously hosted me at a weekend campground owned by another well-connected friend, Zelda Supplee, who apparently knew most of the leading members of the Republican Party in their recreational off moments. A lot of political planning, and hiring, was being done behind the scenes. Present at that same campground, whether by accident or invitation, were Barbara Gittings, who later headed Daughters of Bilitis, and friend.]

Hale was then engaged to marry interracially to William Tatum, a C.O.R.E. co-founder and eventual deputy NYC mayor under Abe Beame. She was in a custody fight with her ex, a member of the powerful Chicago law firm backing McCarthyism. The venue was wrong. Intermarriage was still illegal in many states and Hale was finally forced to give up on Tatum to keep her daughter.

But Hale never gave up on civil rights.

[I have strong reason to suspect that Hale, like a parade of others pre-Watergate whom Nixon may have been desperately trying to protect, may also have been murdered c.1969. By then she had married one of Hoover's lieutenants, Robert Bondi who, if appearances don't lie, may have managed to get hold of Hale's entire estate and have her own daughter disinherited. In my last telephone communication with her just before her demise reportedly of a heart attack, she told me that she was being prevented from leaving the house or even talking to her secretary. I told Porcelain who told everyone else, but nothing was done.]

Thanks to Hale we were all now sleeping with Tigers. Taulman said so. My Viking answer to her was, "We too are Tigers."

Reluctantly, Taulman assented.

ArtemisSmith's ODD GIRL *Revisited*

So now we knew it.

We were positioned to change the system right from the very top. Anointed and protected by Ike, the Commander in Chief, we were giddily building a peace army to tame and re-educate Nixon and all the other Tigers.

[I must have failed to notice how precarious and deeply frightened Taulman felt at the time. She started calling me Tiger, even while reminding me, citing *The Little Prince,* that I was only a Rose with tiny thorns needing to be protected from the Tigers, needing to be put in a bell jar. It was up to her to protect me from the Tigers. But it was she who was the Rose desperately needing bell jar protection, and I didn't see it. Even when she started calling me Poo Bear for poo-pooing everything that was beginning to happen to us and I, still poo-pooing, affectionately was calling her Tigger.]

Gay History books apparently have blindsided this obscure period in the thermidor predating the outbreak of the sexual revolution. With good reason - saying too much about it was dangerous. There really was a war on, and there were many *many* casualties and I wish I could say more, but I'm not the best authority on all the details since I can't remember many names and wasn't attending all of the meetings. Nor was I, as a woman, always included in the innermost circles planning strategy - which is why the female sector soon split and went feminist.

To my eyes, most of the men coming and going tended to look alike. At some point I know must have met Bill Lambert, but I can't remember his face or whether I met him under some other name. And I'm certain Gore Vidal also had to have been there, since his

ArtemisSmith's ODD GIRL *Revisited*

Gay novel, which I bought at the corner candy store back around 1949, long predates mine.

Another important figure in the formative years was R.E.L. Masters, who wrote under a number of pseudonyms and was well-connected on the Democratic side of the civil rights movements although I did not meet him until 1964.

[When we finally did meet, we became good friends even though he had - and rightly so - panned the published *Odd Girl*. Masters changed his mind about my writing when he got to read a sizeable portion of my poetry, novels and plays; this was his advance review on *The Skeets Trilogy:* "As the author presents it, SKEETS is an experimental seduction (or 'rape') of the reader's consciousness, scientifically achieved through esthetic means. SKEETS weaves a strange and compelling tale ostensibly about love and madness - arcane and amoral, atavistic and surreal. ... In both volumes, the narration is unremittingly hypnotic as the author stalks the thought forms she cunningly causes to arise in her relentless and often savage pursuit of 'The Self' and 'The Sacred'. Book I is very well written; Book II, quite remarkable!"]

Masters was a prominent New Age psychotherapist and sexologist. With his wife, theologian and cultural anthropologist Jean Houston, he also co-authored many best sellers including *The Varieties of Psychedelic Experience* which I reviewed for *Science & Mechanics* Magazine in the hope of stopping the spread of LSD.

Despite our ideological differences (my own fields are in the hard sciences - the logic and philosophy of science, psychophysics and information science) Masters and Houston became good friends and sponsors of my work in the arts.

Caught up in the fad surrounding the first discovery of the drug, they had researched the phenomenological effects of psychedelic substances in the 1950's in controlled experiments which had apparently gotten out of hand when the wrong people got hold of them - something altogether too common whenever government-sponsored research meets the Department of Defense.

[Too much has been said about the 1960's sudden flood of narcotics use as a "hippie" and "flower child" rebellion against the Vietnam War. Too little has been said about the sudden availability of drugs and its connection to the late 1950's rise of the civil rights movements. Drugs were the lead weapon in the Mob's war against the arts as the proponents of cultural change. Which mob, you ask? All of them! Cognizant of the real source of the epidemic, I was already waging a militant fight against the spread of LSD and marijuana throughout the 1960's off-off-Broadway café theater scene where by then I was running a prominent anti-war workshop with actors many of whom later won Oscars, Emmys and Obies and some of whom also ran for public office.]

As a best-selling sexologist, Bob Masters' contribution to the Gay Rights Movement has been crucial and he has been unfairly targeted by the anti-Gay establishment, which has openly accused him and his wife, and all their friends, of *witchcraft*. You can go directly to the internet and easily do your own work on researching this shoddy press "expose" which is itself a political witch hunt directed primarily against the Clintons - most probably engineered by very skillful false informants who must have done a snow job on Bob Woodward.

A strong response is called for here: it's important to understand the difference between *immersion* in unconventional research methods and *conversion* in the unconventional forms of life being studied. The former is either play-acting or psychodrama, the latter is serious religious practice.

Both artists and aesthetic researchers indulge in Chaotic Studies, delving deeply into their subjects, but this does not mean they *become* like them. Nor does it make them "witches." *Every* corner of the Human soul is fair game for artistic or phenomenological exploration. How else will physicists and information scientists even begin to ask the questions needed to evaluate the occasional appearance of exotic results?

[Mathematics, pliable and unlimited in all its forms, is a mere tool and not the end-all instrument for reliable explanation. Before a scientific theory can even be formulated, questions have to be generated and framed within some context that lends itself to measurement. Chaotic Studies into the limits of Human introspective experience, an aesthetic (i.e., phenomenological) pursuit, often begins such an epistemological process. Spirits and deities may be invoked, but only to test the limits of the appearances.]

The allegations that Masters and Houston were ever, as *converts*, conducting séances or otherwise engaging in exotic spiritualism or *witchcraft* is just so much misinformed and malicious politically-motivated hogwash! I never attended séances though I'm quite certain they took place - mostly on the liberal Republican side for party entertainment and often frequented by Hale and Porcelain whom I introduced to the Masters who were not themselves the psychics involved, but what is the harm in *anyone's* analyzing such phenomena from more than one perspective?

And might it not even be a proper spiritual investigation for an enlightened leadership? Are the "Reverends" of established "Congregations" the only ones permitted to "counsel" our prospective candidates?

All I found while investigating Masters and Houston over a period of years was harmless cathartic inquiry, aesthetic psychotherapy, which may have valuable 'alternative medicine' applications in the treatment of many pathologies of mind.

And you should take my word for this since I am a thoroughly unconverted skeptic. As an information scientist working on a unified explanatory theory for the phenomenon of self-consciousness, my approach has always been entirely divergent from that of Masters and Houston, but who am I to say whether today's *Fringe* will or will not prompt new explanations to be incorporated in tomorrow's theories?

I should add that, as a sometime stringer for *Science & Mechanics,* back around 1970 I was present and did photograph a session of the therapeutic use of the so-called "Witches Cradle" which was later purchased from me and used in a book authored by John Godwin published by Doubleday & Co.

Who knows whether the research subject in my photos might even have been a young Hillary herself, but again, what if so? It was just a student experiment in what the mind does when it is deprived of its normal proprioceptive parameters. Would *less* knowledge about the workings of her own creative imagination make someone less fit to be President?

[And while I'm at it, let me point out that all highly creative masterbuilders have a right to a strong libido - it comes with the creative territory. All this recent obsession with politicians' private lives is counter-productive and just leads to mediocre replacements.]

ArtemisSmith's ODD GIRL *Revisited*

Dear Colleagues:

Let me backtrack a bit.

In the audience at that first 1954 NYC strategic gathering that now scarcely anyone knows took place, there were a few people already out of the closet whose names are now obscure.

Early press people, interested in covering the Movement but not necessarily Gay themselves, such as freelancers Jess Stearn, John Reavis Jr., Jessica Russell Gaver, and William Carrington Guy of Hearst-owned *Cosmopolitan* later working closely with Helen Gurley Brown, were persons I met soon afterwards and who may have been in the back of the audience.

[Gossip Columnist hopeful Gaver took a special role that I don't see yet listed in *Wickipedia*. A feisty divorcee of the establishment in-crowd - she started a mimeographed newsletter mailed to a very select list of politically-connected readers and established rival columnists, such as Walter Winchell, that targeted anti-Gay commentators in the media by exposing them as closet-gays, thereby adopting Nixon's tactics against his own forces. This was pivotal, since it forced many anti-gay Gays in the Republican camp out of the closet and, by interfering with the established chain of blackmail in the press, also may have helped to bring down Winchell in the process! My source for this was Porcelain, who read her newsletter avidly, and even he was blanched and rendered speechless to repeat its contents and the level of sexual explicitness therein.]

That historical occasion which has up to now apparently escaped GLBT chroniclers was convened by and through announcements in One, Inc., of Los Angeles c.1953, which sent their representative, Ben Tabor - a pretty blonde beardless youth - to address a power audience well beyond the level of his own age and education at a 1500-seat old movie theater then also housing the original Amato Opera on Bleecker Street. The semi-clandestine group of very well-dressed men mostly arrived in couples and were definitely not the type you would see in bars. The handful of women there were not so well-dressed, including *Moi*.

It was standing room only.

The grim and silent audience of mostly angry men became tentatively known as *The League* and its membership later founded New York Mattachine where, while I was in Europe c. 1962, according to its former President Curtis Dewees, for lack of any female participation, I was nominated and unanimously elected vice-president in absentia.

[The founding of NY Mattachine was protracted over a long period of years, beginning c.1955 and stretching into the early 1960's. Taulman and I edited and mimeographed the first newsletter then left the group which became increasingly all-male, and focused our attention on building the local chapter of Daughters of Bilitis, chaired by Marion Glass of either Hunter or Barnard or both, as a feminist community support group.]

ArtemisSmith's ODD GIRL *Revisited*

How many people remember this?
Randy Wicker was in knee pants.

"Saint Mikhail Itkin" who later founded the *Whatever Early Christian Roman Catholic Church*, definitely remembered, but he's dead now and when I knew him he was still a minor calling himself Robin, wearing a red vest to the bars and worshipping Bat Man. (I knew the young Itkin very well and he affectionately called me his cousin and ordained me in absentia, but I distanced myself from him when our conflicting ideologies grew too far apart. I will talk more about him later.)

[There was also someone else - Tony Segura, whom I found most appealing because he looked a lot like Fermi but who, I'm told, went off to Cuba with Fidel. But he may just have been sharing the office that had the mimeograph machine that Taulman and I got to use after hours off of Union Square.]

Among the sparse female presence, mostly c.1953 contributors to *One* Magazine, there were Noel Bustard and Joan Holode, and some middle-aged professional woman, probably a psychologist, sociologist or somebody's mother who many seemed to know but whose name I didn't get, who was immediately voted in as the first *League* Vice President; there was also openly socialist post-racial bisexual Julia Newman who became a good friend of ours though we did not share her political views, and myself, and at later meetings also Taulman.

It was at one of those later (c. 1955-57) formative meetings held at the West End Avenue apartment of first *League* President Gary Kramer (widely-connected *VoxJox* columnist for *Variety),* that I and Taulman, then creative executives in a small advertising agency, first suggested improving the defamatory "Gay" images in the media by initiating a campaign to present more positive portrayals, particularly in advertising commercials -- an art form we knew carried particularly effective subliminal cultural force. I later reintroduced and elaborated on this strategy in the 1960's in my address to the first ECHO (East Coast Homophile Organizations) Conference in Philadelphia.

A friend of Marshall McLuhan's, Edward Daikin (or Dakin) of BBDO, present at that meeting, eagerly took up our suggested strategy and initiated a power meeting of embryonic NY Mattachine with other key media executives for that purpose; though scheduled, it failed to take place.

It was learned some three weeks later that Daikin had been found with his head stuck inside an oven. Suicide, the police determined, over his guilt at being exposed as a homosexual. Bullshit! We all knew it was murder, but could do nothing. The entire movement would have been crushed had we shouted too loudly.

There was definitely a dark side among *The League* and Mattachine membership. Persons who had infiltrated and were there to destroy the Movement. They were the true *Forces of Evil*, a rogue police element that has always been a centuries-old part of the *Mob* and very hard to detect.

There was little we could do about working alongside them except tread as softly and as carefully as possible, suspecting everyone we had not known for years. And even among those persons we knew there might always be a Judas.

Billie Taulman with self-portrait, 1954.

    This period also marked the beginning of my intimate interface with Billie Ann Taulman, who became my creative life-partner of more than fifty years, and whose soul and mine have now become so perfectly intertwined that she continues to this day even in death to be my artistic alter ego.

ArtemisSmith's ODD GIRL *Revisited*

Connecting with each other late in 1954, Taulman and I instantly decided it was Spiritual Love at first sight, but for one small problem: Taulman smoked. I told her that I could never live or work with a smoker, never could be with a smoker. I explained my reasons thoroughly. I told her my whole life story, whereupon she hugged me, told me her own life story and we knew we had finally found each other.

Taulman gave up tobacco on the spot, cold turkey!

Perfectly attuned for creative collaboration, we entered into a civil union in the form of a registered partnership agreement called *Artemis Associates* (not to be confused with a present firm of the same name). We also later took marriage vows: in sickness and in health, for all eternity - although I was still married to Jerry.

Bishop Mikhail Itkin officiated.

We had a party.

Everyone, except family, attended.

But as artists neither of us believed in exclusivity. Nor would either of us ever have been willing to play the traditional role of wife or husband.

[Marriage, even among ordinary people, is such a decadent and useless institution that many persons of all sexes feel it might best be globally eliminated in favor of civil unions! For persons truly in love, marriage is inessential - though it may temporarily be a necessary strategic posture for the Gay Rights Movement to demand that *Marriage* be made legislatively available to everyone.]

In a completely open relationship that welcomed and occasionally included paramours of either sex, we preferred to work and love each other in an entirely new dimension, libido unbound and gender free. Free to wander as we pleased, free to always come home to roost. But by 1959, while being investigated for a possible political career under sponsorship from Hale, the Eisenhowers (and probably Nixon), our professors at Hunter and secretly "Gay" friends among Intelligence personnel now semi-retired and re-employed in academic CIA recruitment, Taulman lapsed into a period of agitated and recurrent paranoia.

It recalled to me all over again what Vilna had gone through post-Fermi in 1943.

But Taulman had a stronger grasp of the situation. She had lived through it in Berkeley, when Republican Nixon on Election Eve had singled out Taulman's group of campaigning New Dealers as "homosexuals and communists" surrounding and supporting Democrat Helen Gehaghan Douglas.

Now Nixon and Hoover were at it again.

Taulman insisted that someone from *The League* had taken her aside and told her we had to be very careful about everything we said to one another, even in private. That we were being bugged my microwaves that could see and hear through walls - something unheard of then, but disclosed post-Watergate in connection with Martha Mitchell's charge that such surveillance technology was killing her. (You should all go Google this, but don't get lost in a whole new research project!)

It's not certain how much of Taulman's breakdown was due to natural causes and how much of it may have been political foul play. Her paranoid fugue was precipitated by a Secret Service investigation while she was being considered for an Assistant position to

ArtemisSmith's ODD GIRL *Revisited*

Eleanor Roosevelt, then United Nations Ambassador working on the Bill for Universal Human Rights.

(Or perhaps all of the tensions generated by the times collided with a flaw in her royal genetic heritage – echoing the madness of King George III!)

Although we should have guessed it, scarcely anyone knew at that time about Hoover's dirty tricks squad and the LSD or other mind-bending substances that were being experimentally introduced into civil rights groups by rogue police factions as a means of interfering with *The League*'s activist activities.

Taulman, marked for greatness, like Daikin only a few weeks earlier may have been one of a number of us simultaneously targeted.

(I was temporarily spared, possibly because everyone might have mistaken Taulman, older and more erudite than I, descended from Mary Ball Washington and so close in likeness to her great-great-great uncle George, may have been identified by McLuhan and others of the group as politically "messianic," and as the real Artemis Smith.)

To this day I cannot tell you how much of Taulman's illness may have been the result of some chromosomal defect misdiagnosed and mistreated through sheer professional stupidity, and how much of it might have been a barefaced bias crime pervasive against all women and gays.

ArtemisSmith's ODD GIRL *Revisited*

Dear Colleagues:

Over the next four years I sold the first-draft of "Anne Loves Beth" along with "Joan of Washington Square" retitled *The Third Sex* to Beacon Books for a combined $1000. (I was also marketing "For Immediate Demolition" retitled *This Bed We Made* c. 1962 for a $1500 advance on further royalties from Monarch Books that I never received, just to get enough money to pay the bills and get Taulman proper treatment which, tragically, proved futile.)

The only competent psychiatric help we were able to find was gratis, from our dear friend Joan McCarthy, a doctoral candidate in Clinical Psychology who, on the eve of her 1963 graduation, died suddenly of a brain abscess. (It's uncertain as to whether it was due to an infected cat scratch to her eye or a gouging at the hands of the female pimp of one of her adolescent clients.)

"Anne Loves Beth" went through a number of revisions before the publishers, rejecting the final version on legal grounds, took the first-draft and blue-penciled it themselves. (Luckily, my contract had stipulated that I owned the copyright!) The 1959 press run for *Odd Girl*, from the very first, was in the hundreds of thousands, with an unreported second printing in the millions, but the publishers never kept open books and all I ever saw was an additional $250 in royalties.

I continued to market the finished "Anne Loves Beth" for eventual hardcover publication. Porcelain and Hale advised me to put it aside for posterity when the teenage market might finally find a place for it.

Being fully committed to writing the first volume of what was later to be *The SKEETS Trilogy*,

ArtemisSmith's ODD GIRL *Revisited*

"Testament of Sarah," which the Hale Agency had presented and committed for sale to Doubleday & Co., I finally put the polished "Anne Loves Beth" to rest.

[Larry Freundlich became my appointed editor and I began revisions and Doubleday hired Stanley Kaufman to write the advance review which was never published. Years later, after Hale's sudden and also suspicious death, the manuscript was returned to me with a form rejection slip, no explanation given.]

Upon the release of *Odd Girl* in 1959 we contacted *The Ladder* and it got excellent reviews. We were invited to attend and speak at a conference in San Francisco. Taulman had sisters in Sacramento she needed to see as well as many friends in Berkeley. We scraped together what money we could, sublet our apartment on 26th Street..

At McCarthy's suggestion I pumped Taulman full of tranquilizers prescribed by Attilio and got her on the plane hoping that perhaps the trip would snap her out of her depression.

It helped a lot, and we got to meet Del Martin and Phyllis Lyon and all the other *Daughters* and had a great time with wonderful people despite Taulman's constant distraction. She was not her shining self. And we also met and consulted with Blanche Baker, Ph.D., who could do little but provide us with a pat on the head and moral support - something rare and precious in those days but not anywhere near the help we got from McCarthy back home.

Everywhere we went, whether in San Francisco to meet Taulman relatives, or Berkeley to meet Taulman friends, or Sacramento to stay with her sisters, or Palo

ArtemisSmith's ODD GIRL *Revisited*

Alto where, at a jazz club called *Upstairs at the Downstairs* managed by our good friend, retired Broadway agent Walter von Behr Teschan, we met and heard Ada Moore, whose identity Billie Holiday may have borrowed at a memorable 1955 concert we caught at *The Village Gate* in NYC, courtesy of *impressario* Trude Heller.

(I didn't have a clue that Holiday wasn't Moore. That's how invisible the "black" community was. What I did know, having become an avid "Moore" fan and having been struck by her tall, strong, frankly "African" pre-*Lion King* style, was that the soft, introverted, *Sarah Vaughn*-like performer sitting at our table in Palo Alto was most decidedly not the same performer I had applauded earlier!)

[Heller, incidentally, was one of the 1950's Gay Bar owners satirized by me as Cora in "Anne Loves Beth." Trude probably never forgave me for the caricature because she later made a special effort to steal all of my best talent in the 1960's for Broadway and Hollywood where they went on to get Oscars, Emmys and so on, leaving me, their director, entirely behind. But Trude wasn't as coarse as Cora, I assure you - she was a very cool lady, and Joel Heller's Mom.]

Taulman had been more deeply into "Black" rights and "Black Culture" than I, having been an account executive to *Carver Federal Savings and Loan* in Harlem. Her portrait of George Washington Carver on their dollar-bill logo blended her own face and that of Carver's. Taulman publicly declared that she was a great-great-grandniece of George Washington and fully believed Carver was her cousin. How our clients loved her up in Harlem! They kept asking for her to come up and work with them and she knew everyone at C.O.R.E. and the NYC office of *Ebony*, and so on, long before I did. She undoubtedly had met Holiday up there earlier.

[George Washington was a very important role model for Taulman as was her "Uncle Earl" (Earl Stanley Gardner) who had been her mother's first love and had made a special trip to NYC to seek her out in hope that he might be her father. Not so, unfortunately.]

In California Taulman was a hero to many and had also been a hero to her younger sisters, who told of her having saved both their lives on numerous occasions on the side of the Sierra Madre where her father, a laid-off Forest Ranger and former Alaskan prospector, ran a snake farm supplying the pharmaceuticals during the Depression. A true descendant of pioneers, Taulman was a dead-eye shot with a rifle and proudly lounged in a coonskin cap, while they told stories of her striding up and down the mountain with them on her back, stepping barefooted over freshly-milked rattlers sunning themselves in their path en route to the local grammar school. Sarah Palin would have adored her!

But that was another Billie. Everywhere we went now, on her own turf Taulman remained in a semi-dream state, compulsively writing down license plates, convinced we were being followed and that it was up to her to protect both of us.

In Sacramento Taulman had strong family support but no one had money. We stayed rent free with her youngest sister Elsie Taulman (a few decades later a

Jeopardy Champion and so much like Billie she might have been her twin) where I managed to find a job as Program and Advertising Manager for KXRQ-FM at a starting advance on commission of $25/week.

But I had neither car nor driver's license and it was hopeless. After a few months of getting nowhere, and the Monarch Books advance not yet forthcoming, I had to ask my father to lend us plane fare home.

[Elsie, incidentally, was employed inside the Pacific Coast industrial complex where she told of the office staff dipping popsicles into vats of liquid oxygen for a special kind of high and playing Poker with plutonium chips until a player's winning streak almost reached a critical mass!]

Returning to our old life and friends and NYC apartment on 26th Street, both of us quickly got freelance advertising jobs but Taulman's agitation grew.

She was never physically violent, but her panic would cause her to hold me prisoner for hours while she subjected me to long tirades about my needing to believe her. I had no choice but to finally give in to the System and put her in Bellevue, where she got assembly-line treatment and was released on medication after six weeks.

On medication she just sat home doing nothing until she stopped taking it and began studying again and working on sparse freelance art assignments, ever so slowly. Meanwhile I went to work 9-to-5 to pay the rent grabbing whatever steady job and freelance assignment I could find, putting my creative career on hold.

By 1961 Taulman's anxieties had subsided and thanks to a friend's recommendation she had finally settled into a rehab job as a layout artist at Mines Press. She was applying to return to Hunter College. Things seemed to be beginning to get back to normal.

By then we were able to get help from an established psychotherapist who obviously meant well but whose advice was so off base that I shall allow her to remain nameless. Together with my parents she managed to convince me that Taulman's dependence on me was complicating her recovery. By then weary and finding myself desperately needing to get back to my own artistic and literary career, I let my parents bribe me into agreeing to work and study in Europe for a year.

Because my parents were paying for the trip and were by now adamant that I quit what everyone in my father's professional circles opined had to be a "co-dependent" relationship, I could not afford to take Taulman along -- but we had made plans for her to secretly join me as soon as she could manage her own plane fare and I could be certain that my student allowance and publishing resources would cover the two of us living as cheaply as one.

When I left NYC Taulman still had a decent job, enough money in the bank to cover about three months' rent, and a roommate who was supposed to sublet the whole apartment whenever she left to join me in Europe.

But too soon after I left, Taulman suffered yet another relapse. Before I could return, our NYC apartment had been dispossessed.

I publish here the last coherent letter I may or may not have received from her. (The original letter is on a sheet too large to reproduce here, but is affectionately preserved among my papers.) To the best of my recollection, it must have reached me in Florence sometime in October 1962 either during or before the Cuban Missile Crisis.

Or perhaps I never received it and it got stuck carelessly among whatever things were salvaged when our apartment on 26th Street was dispossessed during my absence sometime in December 1962. (The period is so filled with grief for me that I can't precisely remember now. What I do remember is that I entirely missed the Cuban Missile Crisis because I was gawking at Florence and not reading newspapers!)

It appears to begin with a handwritten note on the back of a legal-sized well-worn scrapped yellow pulp sheet typewritten on a portable with a tired ribbon that reads:

9/14/62
Lunch @ Work

```
Dearest Tiger -
Thought I should start this now & found this
the only paper available. It comes in rolls @
work. Started @ noon, am now waiting for the
psychologist who might let me into Hunter.
Hope you received my last (rather depressed)
letter. Am having cramps but still worked all
day! They are rather nice there. I'm rather
exhausted.
```

(The paper folds over and adds: "Start here.")

ArtemisSmith's ODD GIRL *Revisited*

Dearest, I am lonely for you and I hope that you will write me nice little descriptions of all the places you visit. What is Picadilly? Who goes there? Everybody? Why? Are you going to visit Soho? You may read this before you go anywhere. Well, you really were willing to reassure me quite a bit before you left, dearest little Tiger. The last page I wrote sounded worse than I meant it to.

Little wiggly friend, no fetish of you will do any good. I converted all that into Tiger-libido long ago. Still need the real, live honest-to-goodness masterful Morpurgo, Right Rhodes. Superb Smith. Even would like to go to a movie with you. It is not true that I am so boring that all I am good for is going to movies with. M. Cosgrove[1] and Persephone[2] keep speaking as though you had gone. Period. At least, M.Cosgrove does. You have flown the coop. And that is it. No more applechop. That I don't really believe?

Spent some time in the Paragon Bookstore on Thursday after I saw that psychologist. I found a beautiful Akkadian dictionary for only $5.00. Also found a Korean grammar for $1.50, and a very deep study of the relationship of Korean to Finno-Ugrian, in dictionary form, for only $5.00. The Assyriac dictionary I found for only $5.00 was interesting, too, with a neo-Babylonian comparison. Then I browsed through a big

---

[1] A 'straight" friend of ours, Margaret Cosgrove, author-illustrator of many children's books and medical texts, whom I entrusted to watch over Taulman and our apartment. When I left for Europe, there was plenty of money in the bank to cover three months' rental and Taulman was employed.

[2] Another 'straight' friend of ours, Persephone Adams, immortalized in a poem written by her father, *New Yorker* editor Franklin P. Adams.

ArtemisSmith's ODD GIRL *Revisited*

Egyptian grammar and dictionary for $45.00 and discovered that it is a very easy language to learn. As far as I can tell, it is very possibly related to Korean. There may be enough here, were I able to acquire all this material, to really verify my hypothesis very nicely. I didn't buy the Egyptian one and see if I can use it at the library in Florence. I might get you to check and see if it is available somewhere there. If you feel like inquiring, ever. Speaking of inquiring, have you stumbled across an introduction to Alice B. Toklas?

It's so strange to be here and well and not have you here hoping with me and being my little Tiger. You wanted us to be self-supporting, and I conked out. Now that there is that possibility again, it seems awful that you are no longer here, too, and that you don't seem to care very much anymore. Perhaps you really do but are too sensitive about everything that has happened to be able to express it. If you did I suppose you would have to blame me, and that you really are reluctant to do a lot of the time. Still, when there is too much burden there is too much.

How about just getting in touch with Alice B. without an introduction? You might say you are a friend of the Interplayers who did her play for a few seasons in California ten years ago. That sounds rather far-fetched as a contact. We worked through her agent, Carl?Van either Doren or Vechten. Which one was her agent, anyway? Can't recall.

For me, frustration is one of the aforementioned burdens. Have been thumbing through back issues of the Ladder in an escapist thing, but that hasn't really helped. Dearest love, little push-cat. It is now 9 p.m. and I have washed the dishes and am getting ready to take a shower and go to bed. I am sorry that I said you didn't care when you more than likely do. Still, it seems that it could be expressed somehow so that I might doubt less. Like "I love you." Very often. Love is never too deep to be expressed when real. Still, one's facilities may fail one temporarily, as mine did when I was sick. They are coming back a little, so you be sure and have me there to express love with them, will you?

Really, I am beginning to enjoy this correspondence. Perhaps as time goes by I will have the strength to include more. Do you know, by the way, how closely the Coptic language is related to ancient Egyptian? I don't.

Dearest little Tiger. I am looking in my little book, "The Roman Forum." It would be wonderful fun to study that with you someday, if you liked. I mean the forum itself. There is an Etruscan inscription there near the tomb of one of the founders of Rome, in something called the "Lapis Niger". It was all covered up by the Romans in the second and first centuries B.C. Maybe the Etruscans had more to do with the founding than anyone liked to admit. They really "covered up." They used a pavement of black Greek marble. I love you.

It is now time for me to clamber over Antigone and go to bed. I will take a bath in the morning. I will be a slob tonight and not do so. Hope you get in touch with Tim Courtney. She was a brilliant student at Cal. In English, I think. Meanwhile, dear Tiger, tell me about the nice people you meet. If you can, tell me how much you love me. That will help. You are my dear love, my sweet love. I need you and I hoope that you will need me so much soon that you will want me to come early.

It is interesting that the thumb-screws are still on at Hunter even though you have gone to Europe. That didn't seem to prove or defend anything to this psychologist from the Dean's office who put me through the two-hour grill session.

Tiger, tiger. Where are you tonight? What little dreams did you have on shipboard that you will tear up and not tell me. What dreams are you living now? They are really mine, too. I want you to write them to me, whether they happen sleeping or waking.
Isobel Aronin[3] called. She has lost her job. They weren't nice, made false accusations about her competence. She is most unhappy. See what happens the minute you go? The world

---

[3] Another 'straight' friend of ours, then an editor at *Scribner's*, who had just sponsored the submission of one of my manuscripts there.

ArtemisSmith's ODD GIRL *Revisited*

just isn't the same, somehow.

Dearest, dearest, dearest. Antigone and I miss you. I will go to sleep now, hoping that I will see you in January. **Meanwhile, I dreamed last night that you were hanging a cat by its toes and I went and took it down.** It was a comfort to be near you even though your behavior was not the kindest in the world. In fact, I was very happy to be near you in the dream.

I am wearing your nice steel wristwatch, thinking that you would want me to. Would you like me to send it?

All my personal nightingales have stopped singing now that you are gone, dearest. Perhaps I can find a mechanical one somewhere that will cheer me up for a while. The teachers in my classes. Still.
    All my love, my passion, my tender love,

Billie

Billie

[On the back of the same page, there seems to be a letter written either earlier or later:]

Sunday night .. . . 5 P.M. Much has happened since I last wrote, but little has been accomplished. The psychologist who saw me said that he would have the medical board pass on me after I was at Hunter for a bit. I am disgusted. He asked me (without prompting)

ArtemisSmith's ODD GIRL *Revisited*

all about Dr. Thompson,[4] grilled me, asked me if my left-hand ring was a wedding ring. I told him it was given me by someone at Yale. He asked then if it were a man, and seemed dubious when I said "yes." It was very, very nasty, and it certainly would be nice to take that last year in England rather than here. It was long and grueling and I was having severe cramps. Didn't recover until just now. Had them for two days. Then Persephone came over and refused to pay the two-month's rent in advance and browbeat me et al. Then she called today and apologized, saying that her mother had tried to convince her that my demands were not unreasonable. I had asked for rent in cash, so I wouldn't have to accept a check from her lawyer. So now she may give me a month's rent in advance. I find these hostile hesitations very tiring. She began to feed me a tirade about how I might go insane, saying you had told her about my violence toward you and my "catatonic stupors" and this and that. All this so that she might not have to pay that month's rent in advance. Now, however, her tone has changed completely.

Then I spent yesterday afternoon with M. Cosgrove, who was very nice and took me to her Community Center briefly, then took me home and had me lie down while she did

---

[4] Possibly an administrative 'plant' set up at Hunter by the early CIA/FBI or Secret Service to check Taulman out by attempting to seduce her. I later encountered a similar woman in the 1960's and '70's under a number of different academic identities, when she unsuccessfully targeted me. Such 'traps' were regularly employed, especially within the military but also among academics being investigated for security clearances. The persons employed for such purposes were themselves victims of military blackmail, so I continue to decline to name her. I hope someday she will come forward herself.

ArtemisSmith's ODD GIRL *Revisited*

sewing. It was very amusing, and we had shrimp salad. Thank God for M. Cosgrove. She talked to me about you at length, was very sympathetic and understanding.

I am very frustrated. Where are you, little Tiger? Where? Where? Looked in the magazine rack, refrigerator, bed, back room, bathroom. No tiger. No Tiger. Antigone is rummaging around the closet looking for something. She probably misses you too.

Did you tell me not to ask Persephone rent in advance? She has only stored her stuff for three months, so may move, etc. I thought I was supposed to speak to her about it. By the way, I'm so glad you finally took care of those library books. You really should have let me pay the $1.50 or so we owed originally, as I suggested. It might have been $5.00. Ah weell. I should berate you? Poor little tiger. You were having enough troubles then. I love you.

Dearest little pussycat. If you see something in a Gunn plaid there, perhaps you should get Dr. Wilson.[5] a small souvenir. I haven't gotten in touch with her about taking her to <u>Antigone</u>. I suppose I should before she makes other arrangements. Still, now that you

---

[5] Celebrated Classics Professor Pearl Cleveland Wilson who, along with Classics and English Department Heads Adelaide Hahn and Leah Jonas, had fondly assigned us the star names of 'Castor and Pollux' because we dressed alike, in army surplus fatigues, in defiance of the Roman Catholic-run highly conservative History Department on the same floor who regularly complained about our unisex attire to the Dean's Office. We got away with it by counter-charging religious persecution, as 'devout atheists', and daring the administration to risk a lawsuit on First Amendment grounds.

are gone the energy fails me. I feel very withdrawing and hostile and unhappy. There is no real point in social life. No real point in anything, for that matter. Don't be contemptuous. I may be right. Following as one is led by the requirements of travel, school, et al, is not the same as having real purpose and fulfilling that purpose. That is why schoolwork is not regarded as seriously as post-graduate or independent work. So I reach sycophantic heights of expressed eulogy and get good grades in all my courses .… so then I will be known as having done that. Well and good. But when my little fellow student, the real inspiration of all my independent work, has gone, there is not much there. Seriously. I still value my mate as my inspiration. When it is gone or it is no longer mutual, I do not pretend that the mechanical data provided by an ordinary college education, sugared up with a dramatic presentation, can fill that gap. It may be that there is more left of our relationship than you had led me to believe. I still have that hope. But you are not here to feed the hope (though you had not the desire to confirm it entirely when you were here) and much depends upon your letters. That is different from dependency, however. It simply is love. Without it there is no love. Demand and response are part of a mutually nonschizophrenic relationship. When one asks a question, an answer is expected. When this happens, that happens. One treats one's friend nicely. Expectations are fulfilled. All that. It's all a part of a unit that's a little like a beautiful plant, when parts of the plant are clipped it's easy to see whether someone has snipped off the buds or taken only the old, tired flowers. The gardener can talk his head off about his purity of purpose and what his schedule was when he was trimming the plant, but those are

ArtemisSmith's ODD GIRL *Revisited*

rather extraneous factors in love. The only
schedule the plant of love has is regular
watering with the milk of human kindness.
Sounds awfully exotic. Like taking baths in
asses' milk.

I won't be able to get physical education in
this time. It starts too soon. It takes me
forty minutes to get from work to class, via
subway. Where is the milk of human kindness
for the lovable little tiger to get in this
letter? I'd better start churning some up and
serving out some yogurt. Only when there is
some of you in the idea I am discussing is
there anything that is really nice. I guess I
will try and take the full twelve units.
There is an English course by Professor
Bowden, "The Structure of Modern English,"
that fits in beautifully with my schedule, so
that could make up the additional units and
be very worthwhile. Sounds like a good
grammar course, and we all need that.
(see back of page)

* * * * * * *

Our friends lied. I never broke up with Taulman - quite the opposite. After only four weeks in 1962 I had abruptly ended a lucrative career engagement to an academic so well off and so entirely in love with me that he would have been willing to accept Taulman's permanent presence in our lives and support both of us.

I did so simply because I could no longer bring myself to live that kind of life. Taulman was by then my wife, for better, for worse, even though the *for worse* part needed a lot of work.

Taulman had her first breakdown in 1957; by 1962 we had pretty much run out of options. Separation, to end Taulman's dependency on me (as revered and established Dr. Nameless had opined), was the last psychiatric recommendation still to be explored.

My own career was running down the tubes. I was ready but still unwilling to cut the cord, by then finding myself suddenly fired from every career job I applied for and driven to support us by working in various menial capacities ranging from Dictaphone transcription in a secretarial pool to nude modeling for artists and their students. All our friends except McCarthy (temporarily absent because in hospital with an infected eye injury) were by now intervening and I was being made to feel like some kind of alcoholic in need of rehab. The trip to Europe would have helped both of us turn the page - and I had really made every realistic preparation for her to join me.

And I had entrusted M. Cosgrove with the charge of keeping me posted, but I wasn't told of Taulman's relapse until it was too late even to fly back; and Cosgrove assured me that it had all happened so fast that immediately returning would be futile.

Simultaneously Vilna, who had always viewed Taulman as a rival, cunningly was already on the boat to join me in Rome for a professional power tour to old Partisans now anxious to meet both of us. Letters carried with her from other trusted friends further assured me that catching the first plane back would be to no avail - Taulman was getting proper treatment and all of our treasured belongings had already been put safely into storage.

But Taulman did not get proper treatment, and before the moving van hired by M. Cosgrove got there

ArtemisSmith's ODD GIRL *Revisited*

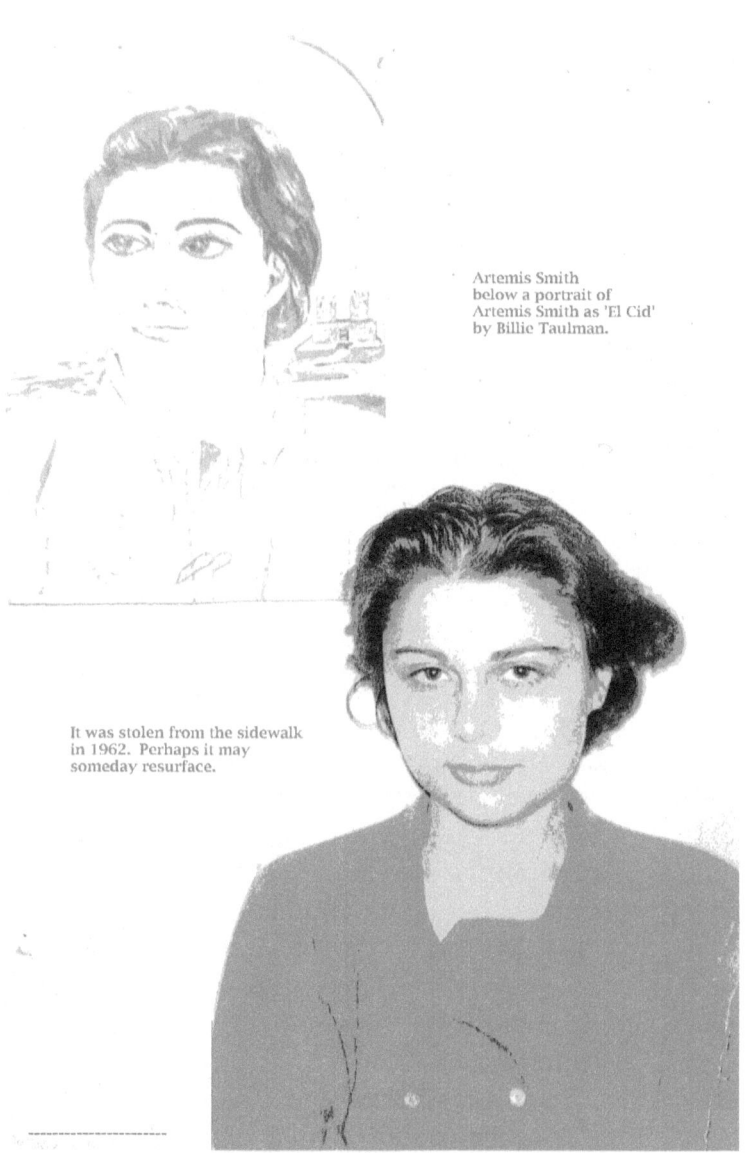

Artemis Smith
below a portrait of
Artemis Smith as 'El Cid'
by Billie Taulman.

It was stolen from the sidewalk
in 1962. Perhaps it may
someday resurface.

only a fraction of our property remained on the sidewalk, the most valuable pieces having been "rescued" by foraging lesbian couples who eventually ended up keeping most of Taulman's collection of modern paintings and first editions for themselves while I, too grief stricken to demand their return, simply went on with my own life.

.   But I wouldn't let go.

I hustled Vilna back on a boat in Naples after only a short stay then dropped out of the University of Rome and shortened the rest of my scheduled professional tour, rushing back only to find myself rejected and medically barred from visiting Taulman again "in her best interest for recovery."

One way or another she must have been brainwashed. She had started smoking again and said she had found a new lover and that it was alright now for me not to worry about her.

I sat there helpless, unbelieving. Had I read the letter she had sent me, weary as I was I might have pressed more strongly to have her released in my own care. I did have attorneys, notably William J. Calise who was helping Gays, that I could have called but didn't. There might also have been Hale's attorney, Philip Wittenberg, but I didn't think of him.

By then McCarthy, on whom we so desperately relied for insight and resource, *alas* was suddenly no more and I, alone, was worn too thin to oppose the system psychiatrists. I did not know then what I know now about brain architecture and chemistry. Today I could have done better but at that time I was wholly dependent upon well-meaning but theoretically disinformed Dr. Nameless in consult with what may have been an army of biased and politically corrupt and antiquated professional opinions.

And Taulman's smoking really did it for me. That was the final cut.

Still I decided not to give up on her, but to give both of us needed time apart. Creatively, artistically, we were too close, perhaps toxic to each other. Just as Vilna and I could not long exist in the same space.

Perhaps as Dr. Nameless had assured me, Taulman was incurable. For years I had tried to heal her on my own, simply with love, understanding and much patience but to no avail. Perhaps she was beyond all psychotherapy. Perhaps intensive mind-fracturing medication rendering her only half the person she had been was the only solution. Perhaps the real Taulman was no more and would never return. Perhaps all my friends and family were right and I really should get on with my own career, sing my own song without accompaniment, be the real and only Artemis Smith.

Watching closely from afar, I entrusted her care to M. Cosgrove, herself a versatile and highly creative person who appeared to know more than I did and was right there, ready to step up to the plate.

The motives for Cosgrove's readiness to do so still remain a mystery to me, since she was totally heterosexual, but Taulman was still such a poetic presence that perhaps spontaneously Cosgrove wanted to be near her, as I had, even if only for personal and spiritual growth.

Even in her most distracted condition Taulman

was amazing. Her daily insights into the very fabric of Being were unique and unparalleled. At times each sentence she uttered burned with the proverbial *hard gem-like flame* of immortal prose. It's difficult to describe the experience of being close to her except by saying, simply, that basking in her radiance was for everyone touched by her an experience of *becoming Taulman*. She repeatedly pinpointed and expressed one's inner word. No wonder Cosgrove was eager to take charge of her! And I, deprived of her, deeply felt the void.

And Cosgrove, too, was also such a brilliant and mercurial person that both I and Taulman had fallen in love with her at first sight. So we now eagerly allowed her to manage us. Taulman had become the Rose now being kept safe in Cosgrove's bell jar, safe from me and all the other Tigers.

So Cosgrove became Taulman's "committee" during this period and took over for me while Billie spent the next five years as an in patient and out patient at Wards' Island, until my career took a positive turn and I finally gathered myself together and stepped forward to reclaim her -- this time to be welcomed by a new generation of medics and social workers standing with open arms.

Where had I been! She needed me!

I took her back then, tobacco and all, though just as with Vilna I never could come physically close to her again. For as long as Taulman continued to smoke we would have to live apart.

Having for years anticipated her eventual release from hospital, I had sublet and kept my old $65/month rent-controlled walkup ready for her to move into; it was only a couple of blocks from my new $200/month luxury studio on 72nd Street where I would see her every day when she came to eat with me.

I would cook magnificent holistic meals for her, I would pump her full of vitamins, I would make certain she was safe and wouldn't relapse, even though by then I had a succession of primarily female paramours living with me, each of them fully understanding and never resenting her presence in my life. All of them knew why I could never *ever* love anyone as I had loved Taulman again.

(My survivor guilt during that period forms the resounding theme of *The SKEETS Triptych*. But I nevertheless found positive ways to move on without precisely leaving Taulman behind. I will reserve filling you in on that part of my very long life for some other edition.)

As for my own possessions that had also been left on the street in 1962, Ida was that day dying in hospital and Vilna and Attilio couldn't stop by for them. My sister and brother-in-law grudgingly rescued only what they deemed important to the family, leaving the rest on the street for the storage van hired by Cosgrove that arrived too late.

Fortunately, I had taken many of my manuscripts with me, but the final draft of "Anne Loves Beth" was not among them. (I had been afraid to take it with me lest it be confiscated as possibly salacious material on my return through Customs!)

ArtemisSmith's ODD GIRL *Revisited*

Billie Taulman by Artemis Smith. 1969

ArtemisSmith's ODD GIRL *Revisited*

Dear Colleagues:

"Anne Loves Beth" included in an earlier edition and now also published separately as *"ArtemisSmith's* ODD GIRL Restored" is a faithful reconstruction from memory of that earlier revised version.

It is now made available primarily to librarians and academics for historical purposes and possibly also finally for teen libraries.

It cannot really be narrowly classified as either a *gay* or *lesbian* novel, never should have been. Its political stance and psychological views are diametrically opposite to the portraits of "gay life" in transgender comic renditions exploited by the mass media for their commercial value.

Dated as *Odd Girl* may read today, now that wholesome alternative life-choices among consenting adults is a legal and socially acceptable category, I maintain it rightfully stands as a serious work of literature specifically aimed at guiding the young away from the hurdles that await them upon 'coming out' in what, for most of the world, is still unavoidably an underworld environment.

ArtemisSmith's ODD GIRL *Revisited*

Especially for female adolescents voraciously seeking knowledge of an alternate lifestyle that does not utterly misguide them, it still stands as an honest study in the phenomenology of androgyny that may facilitate their self-knowledge and natural sexual development -- even though my character, Anne, now may sound more like Nancy Drew on an estrogen overdose!

But this was exactly what I originally meant Anne to be, speaking directly to all the *'odd girls'* who desperately needed positive teenage models back in 1954. Though tame by comparison to other pulp fiction published today, for its time *Odd Girl* was unavoidably explicit, as a frank work of literature should be -- unlike its companion piece, *The Third Sex*, which was a hastily-written disguised activist statement specifically aimed at reaching a wider multinational heterosexual audience.

Never intended as a literary work of art except in the larger sense of political 'master-building' for social change, *The Third Sex* intentionally contained no sexually explicit passages that might have prompted censorship and confiscation, and was written more as a journalistic essay than as a novel, specifically for the purpose of tapping the powerful global pulp fiction mass medium that was, in those days, the only ready podium for the sexual minorities' rights activism.

In 1959, my shock and outspoken outrage at the publisher's offensive blurbs on the cover of O*dd Girl* – describing it as a portrait of life and love among "warped women" – widely reverberated throughout the gay community in their many newsletters and publications, notably *The Ladder,* successfully putting sufficient pressure on my publishers to immediately release *The Third Sex* with almost no editorial change. (Initially meant to be a collaboration, Taulman only ended up writing one chapter. The one offensive editorial insertion was the subtle interjection of after-sex smoking, as well as other smoking references. I never wrote or approved those lines - and I wonder if Taulman sneaked them in or one of the editors did.)

A line in the sand was gradually being drawn: *The Third Sex* was presented as a portrayal of both male and female gay society in a positive and humanist light. Riding on the prior success of *Odd Girl*, it became one of the key source materials of the 1960's rights movements. It spoke the truth for a precise time and place and is now also a piece of history. For this reason, I see no reason to revise it even though, as a novel, it is inferior and artistically thin. A revised edition would cure its literary defects, but why bother?

Not so however for *Odd Girl* alias "Anne Loves Beth." In its finished form it can still present an important contribution to the understanding of the complexities of the female mind in adolescence. The final draft contributes both to the phenomenology and the psychology of the developing female persona.

Suppressed by society and by my pulp publishers, this offering was never given a fair chance and should now be presented in its true light for it is important to realize that, despite the rise of feminism, theories regarding the female adolescent libido still continue to be largely formulated and defined by male academic professionals groping to understand what they cannot possibly experience themselves -- and the checkbooks of male-oriented media pornographers, even when they happen to be written or directed by women.

Compare my message to that of other contemporary writers of "lesbian pulp fiction" and see the difference.

Odd Girl alias "Anne Loves Beth," as a product of my uninhibited phenomenological investigation into the depths of my own adolescent psychic development, presented a consciousness-raising alternative that many young women may secretly experience but fearfully suppress to their own detriment. It sought to lead such young women toward making more educated life choices - and not necessarily gay choices. In this sense, pulp fiction too can be an aesthetically valid art form.

Despite its clay feet, "Anne Loves Beth" is contiguous with the rest of my master-building investigations into the metaphysics of Gender Being. I continue to be a cultural revolutionary now writing primarily under the sci-fi category, sketching hypotheses that Humanity may still not yet be fully ready to accept.

[Books II and III of *The SKEETS Trilptych* speak to that side of me as well as my upcoming "*ArtemisSmith's* GrandmaMoseX:*the Final Testament before the Apocalypse.*"]

The sci-fi futurist vision of a strictly gender-free identity is inseparable from my *mystical-atheist* conviction that Human evolution beyond its present species level presents us with unbounded territories for superhuman expansion that really do need to be morally contained, but in a new key if we are to remain *Human* rather than *Vampire*, *Insect* or *Borg*.

Biologically-based existence, still now for us

ArtemisSmith's ODD GIRL *Revisited*

essentially earth-bound, is merely pupal. Soon it will metamorphose into forms better suited for interstellar exploration, hopefully *Angellic* forms that are free in every sense and limited only by the ethical, the moral, and the beautiful for the preservation of our original and most valuable Human identity.

It is time to throw out viral and superstitious old Scripture and its pathological applications, time to set all of us free to be all that we really can become.

To those who would ridicule me for stooping to write pulp fiction as an art form, I say you are short-sighted. I was only paid a pittance for my writing and could have made much more had I really been willing to become a literary hack within the establishment media.

But my artistic goals were much wider: my pulp fiction titles then, as well as my sci-fi titles now, consciously and strategically took advantage of a mass medium quite possibly still thoroughly controlled by the vast underworld anti-culture. I have always used one of the fringe industries of those all-permeating forces of evil to sneak through a positive socio-political message that could not be presented through normal channels.

And I see this as literary master-building at its purest -- my chosen form of urban-guerrilla-warfare turned against the very mob that still seeks to oppress vast sections of humanity - including even persons occupying the highest echelons of political leadership - through blackmail, extortion, and prostitution.

In the 1950's, both Taulman and I saw that the fight for Gay rights was more than just an advocacy for the human rights of a small segment of the population. Historically this portion of the politically disenfranchised minorities have always been the unwilling handmaidens of organized crime at all its levels - as were the politically-oppressed 'rich' Jews during the early rise of Hitler.

All persons secretly living alternate life-styles form not a minority but the proverbial global silent majority.

As first publicly stated by us and repeated throughout our artistic careers, in this country, as in any other country, there can be no human rights for women or any of the racio-ethnic minorities without first also including the rights of all persons in alternate life-styles. Their representation is not only morally but also strategically crucial: *wherever one group of persons is rendered subject to control by organized crime through lack of rights legislation, the entire society is threatened, the whole world is threatened.*

This was why both Taulman and I gave Gay activism first priority even over Feminism and Interracialism. And this was also why the death squads of the rogue police establishment may eventually have put both of us on their hit lists.

There is much more to tell you here and at my online interlocking websites-- but now I simply call your scholarly attention to "Anne Loves Beth" which, despite its 1950's setting, in many parts of the world may still forcefully address the present.

ArtemisSmith's ODD GIRL *Revisited*

Dear Colleagues:

Have I still got your attention? Is anyone still reading? *Hallelujah!* Since the 1980's when I lost the remainder of my closest sounding boards to one form of cancer or another I have been writing in a virtual vacuum.

Taulman survived until 2008 but it was mostly her insights, not mine, that got to bounce back and forth between us. Taulman has been my prophet all these years and make no mistake about it - we are *both* writing this now, though now that she is gone I am finally free to talk about all the things *I* have had to leave unsaid until the cock crowed.

In order for you to understand what took place in our lives and the lives of others who touched us during the 1960-70's, I will have to go back again briefly to a time before I met Taulman, to 1952.

ArtemisSmith's ODD GIRL *Revisited*

I and Michael Itkin, or little Robin as I used to call him, found each other at or in the San Remo, a gay corner bar on Bleecker and McDougal. That area got so crowded at night that all of the partying spilled out into the street and the underaged set found it easy to mix with the grownups without precipitating a police raid.

(My own hangout was at the Café Rienzi a few doors down which had become my alternate office whenever I was not at the Hale Agency on West 10th. There I once met and spoke at length with Jack Kerouac who convinced me *not* to go on the road with my husband Jerry.)

I would repeatedly pass by the San Remo and stop to chat with Robin between my matinee and nightly gigs at the Amato Opera and The Provincetown Players. Itkin and his friends became my principal source for the composite character called 'Jacques' in "Anne Loves Beth" and for a while we had much in common.

Religion was the unifying factor, our mutual rage and contempt for its political presence and interference in both our lives - I then as Feminist, he then as Gay. Both of us were talking about the need to start our own religion to oppose all the dogma that was out there. Doing so was only one of my remote future projects, but for Itkin it became an immediate and growing obsession to a degree that I, as politically anti-Vatican and down on all hope of salvaging its fundamental tenets, personally regarded as futile.

But instead of staying in school and getting all the higher degrees for which his high intelligence should have easily qualified him, Itkin slipped deeper and deeper into his own mystical calling despite all of my efforts to talk sense into him and even to introduce him to the right kind of Bat Man to take him in hand.

It was a stage he never outgrew.

Though I still look upon all such religious dogma as misguided, St. Mikhail's courageous contribution to the Gay Rights Movement undeniably has had strategic importance and he really should be canonized by the Vatican as one of its martyrs whenever the Pope or one of his successors decides to have his/her next epiphany.

By his very manner, appearance and costumed ritual which he jokingly began as a kind of transgender 'drag', Itkin exposed the sham in all the organized religions he mimicked. (Thinking back, looking at how fondly he unwrapped and unfolded his colorful vestments I am always reminded of what was later stunningly satirized in Fellini's *Juliet of the Spirits* in what appears to be an authentic Vatican fashion show where male models wearing the latest fashions in High Mass and Papal attire parade down the runway in a frankly transgender display!)

The sad thing is that when it all began, and it probably began during a conversation had between the two of us in 1952, I was only half listening. He was talking about Jesus and the Apostles possibly having all been Gay, and I was countering that with the observation that gender-freedom was clearly outlined in Plato's *Republic* with its notion of the "philosopher king" who might be either male or qualifying female and that had largely formed the basis for subsequent Early Christian thought.

ArtemisSmith's ODD GIRL *Revisited*

There really is a need, we both concluded when we were actually listening to each other and not going off on our own separate monologues, to reform all the religions to allow for both gender-freedom and gender equality.

I really did see it as nothing more than a Gay Rights counter-Vatican parody. When it finally hit me that he was dead serious about running for sainthood over this, I gave up on him and went my own artistic way but Itkin on that day apparently took me seriously, went out and incorporated his first *Whatever* Church then sent me a diploma ordaining me in absentia as one of his ministers which I laughingly tossed in some pile of papers and eventually threw out.

(To my mind all "Holy Books" belong either in the fire or in the back of some dusty library never to be consulted by anyone but historians and cultural anthropologists. Even philosophers should avoid them lest they pick up a spiritual virus they had best not propagate! The Vatican, incidentally, held the same view in the Middle Ages, when it actively forbade any translation of the Bible into the vernacular.)

The way I saw it, Itkin started his movement as a means of *politically* fighting fire with fire. But it soon afflicted him *spiritually* as it later did too many young men damaged by their own religious upbringing who seriously sought and found refuge in the Early Christian Roman Catholic or *Whatever* Church's Vatican alternative.

One pathology of soul can never properly heal another. Yes, I dare use the word *pathology*. While a minor, Itkin was victimized despite all his protestations to the contrary, either by a devout priest or a depraved predator; take your pick, there is no difference between them where minors are concerned. Man-boy love, unless it is *entirely* non-sexual, is statutory rape no matter what you call it.

But so is early-childhood religious indoctrination *a rape of the soul* and Itkin was apparently subjected to both. Like most of the gay virgins of Itkin's crowd, it left him obsessed with sado-masochist symbolism and an irresistible urge to either engage in Black Masses or otherwise expose and act out his fantasies.

To Itkin I was always a neutral and understanding female presence providing the needed family acceptance he could not find at home. *Ergo* his insistence on assisting me but only if he could do it naked. Why not! Being always unaffected by a show of male nudity, I simply went on with my own tasks and let Itkin get through his own hang ups as we worked. (And he had quite a number of hang ups he has never minded telling the whole world about so I don't think I am breaking any confidence by setting them down for posterity here.)

I can't remember precisely what he told me about his Jewish-Catholic childhood in the Fordham area of the Bronx that fated day in 1952 when he eagerly volunteered to help me paint the ceiling of my new basement apartment on East 17th. (A firehouse red, which I lived to regret!) He insisted I allow him to do it stark naked, despite my warning on the possible harmful effects of applying paint thinner on a penis. (Which he, to his agony, also learned to regret that same day!)

I was more interested in what I had to tell him

about my own, however brief, Roman Catholic upbringing and in what ways it had corrupted me.

As you may recall, back in 1934 Protestant (and excommunicated-sometime-Bolshevik) Vilna had to promise to have her "biracial" Aryan-Hebrew children baptized and raised under the protection of Pope Pius XI in order to expedite her civil marriage to Freemason Attilio.

After both my sister and I were born, Vilna continued to delay and delay on her extorted promise, but by 1937 the Pope was offering the Jews his special protection and Vilna finally gave in. She permitted our baptism. Our newly hired maid Celeste, of dubious origin (Vilna, a pushover for hard-luck stories, had probably hired her off the street without references to keep her out of prostitution), was instructed to take us to church for indoctrination by her parish priest, a stern, evangelistic sort who was hell-bent on converting Jews into Catholics with threats of Hellfire if they did not learn better ways.

(The magnificently illustrated volume of Dante's *Inferno* by Auguste Doré, a copy of which was also in Vilna's studio, was apparently his favorite children's book, and he had a stick inside his gown that got larger and more menacing everytime he took me on his lap to lecture me about Satan and his brood, Doré in hand.)

In contrast, our own emissary to and from the Vatican had been a benign family friend, *Padre* Capitani, with no parish of his own - a little fellow very much like Itkin later became, living in abject poverty, poetically and artistically inclined. That kind of priest is a prize! No objections to him.

ArtemisSmith's ODD GIRL *Revisited*

For years the *Padre* had brought Old Masters back and forth from the Vatican for Vilna to copy or clean or restore and had received food and medical treatment from Attilio for himself and whomever miserable creature from the street he brought to our door.

As a four-year-old watching Mamma work, I was constantly being exposed to all the art projects brought to her at once, stacked against the wall - usually gory religious art of torture and crucifixions and once in a while a Bosch filled with visceral monstrosities.

(To save on colors all-too-quickly drying up on her palette, Vilna would simultaneously work on Vatican copies or restorations and her own canvases on separate easels.)

Attilio's books of medical drawings as well as our own volume of Doré's *Inferno*, were also lying around always open to some dissection detail or demonic page, for Vilna's anatomical or design cross-reference.

Vilna's Lutheran childhood, against which she had totally rebelled, had long-deconditioned her to the graphic nature of such relics and like Mamma I too had become accustomed to looking at all that work analytically, not for the horror it depicted but for its anatomical accuracy in depicting it. Both of us were blinded as most children in religious communities become blinded through repeated exposure - that is, until Attilio reminded Vilna to point out to me the actual outrage depicted in such scenes, for he as a physician was still greatly sensitized to it.

(It was mostly Attilio who kept reminding me through the years that such sights were actually real and deplorable. He would also tell of his experience and outrage as a physician often called to monasteries and nunneries to treat or declare persons dead who had voluntarily immured themselves in shallow coffin-size cubicles where they were allowed to waste away lying in their own excrement in so-called "mystical" catatonic stupor.)

But such sensitization at home now blended with "religious instruction" at Church and a bite from the apple of the tree of knowledge abruptly evicted innocent me, no longer *God-favored Adam* but *God-accursed Eve* from paradise. Suddenly, Doré's *Inferno* became real to me and all the agonies of the martyrs blended with the hellfires of tortured souls. And now also according to our parish priest, *souls tortured by God Himself!*

(His half-crazed disciple, Celeste, much too anxious to reinforce his teachings, had meanwhile simultaneously grown into the *Nanny-from-Hell* whenever our parents were away, pretending to play with us while acting as the Devil after our souls. My desperate phone call to my mother during one of those episodes finally convinced my parents to let her go. Tearfully she left us without references and was probably forced to become a prostitute after all!)

Celeste banished and her priest along with her, the nightmares nevertheless persisted. Vilna was forced to deprogram me. She would shake me awake saying "You are not in Hell! Come with me, we are going to Heaven!"

Fortunately it didn't take much for Vilna to bring me back to normal even though she herself had been more permanently damaged.

She had likewise been violated by Lutheran zealots and all their threats of Hellfire which would sometimes creep back into her mind causing nightmares despite her mature decision to renounce her faith. She had turned to mysticism, first to one, then another, then another variety. She was deeply religious though thoroughly anti-Church of any kind and saw Christ as wholly disembodied and symbolical.

(When as a child I asked her how to draw an anatomically correct Christ, she said Christ was both Human and an Angel. And when I asked her how to draw an anatomically correct Angel, she said Angels do not have bodies. There was no anatomically correct way to draw either Christ or any of the Angels, although all of them were Human in form. This was most puzzling to me until I arrived at my own creed. But *now* I finally understand what she meant.)

So all of this was what I was telling Itkin while he was trying to get his early-childhood hang ups off his own chest. (By then we had finished painting the ceiling red, and I already knew it had been a big mistake, but too late!)

We paused, then he agonized over having to apply the paint-thinner wincing and joking all the while about mortifications of the flesh while I made us dinner. And by then he had his clothes on but insisted on staying long enough to read me passages from the Marquis De Sade and his own poetic embellishments on them which I found totally uninteresting.

I was completely turned off but let him ramble on, realizing that he desperately needed to unload all this woman-hating crap on someone female but not judgmental, and I was his only family.

It was his developmental need.

I knew he would outgrow it, which he did.

I also permitted him to elicit a promise from me that I would let him conduct a Black Mass under my new red ceiling - which I did on a Halloween, inviting all the Fordham graduates hanging around Porcelain and Alfred Hitchcock at The Mystery Writers Guild, and the party became a precursor of the *Rocky Horror Picture Show* nearly two decades before the cult classic.

There was no doubt in my mind that all this prolonged though thoroughly innocent and cathartic fascination with satanic subjects, both by Itkin and the Fordham set, was the result of their having been victimized by their religious education.

That the Fordham boys cleansed and sublimated their fantasies by writing successful movie and television scripts while Itkin remained obsessed with becoming a priest in his own religion shows the many forms of adjustment to such victimization that takes place when boys, who will be boys, finally grow up.

But what all of this only goes to show is that pederasty comes in more than one form and should in all instances be restrained. This was the important insight we both came away with that day in 1952.

Despite our widely divergent approaches, Itkin and I (and later also Taulman and I) arrived at the conclusion that *any* religion that gets hold of the young before they have a chance to develop their minds to think critically and impartially, in its hunger to recruit and indoctrinate with so-called Holy Books and liturgy, should be legislatively barred from doing so.

Freedom of religion should never be seen as a license to corrupt the young.

In the years that followed, both of us in our own way carried this notion forward as we moved separately through the various Rights Movements. And Itkin's contribution is by no means slight.

Because of him the Vatican, as well as all other antiquated edifices, may soon have to change many of their fundamental tenets or risk total structural collapse under the weight of increasing scientific evidence that whatever is meant by the notion of 'eternal life' may indeed be entirely achievable in *this* world rather than in the next.

But first there must be global ideological emancipation.

Today, adequate legislation protecting the young from the pathology of ideology is still sorely lacking. To my mind, the most important step in that direction would be not merely to tax but to boldly outlaw all religious schooling until after high school. Doing so would simultaneously bolster the public education system and permit a stronger emphasis in science, technology and the humanities.

Religion, like sex, can wait until the young have a chance to grow up and think for themselves.

Again to my mind, in the final analysis anyone who holds St. Mikhail in contempt must also hold the

Pope and all his radical priests in contempt, for corrupting *all* the young both gay and straight, and must also hold every radical Imam and every radical Rabi similarly in contempt, for there is no difference among them.

Guys, is it a deal? Zero tolerance for the corruption of the young either sexual or spiritual. Public education and *only* public education before the age of eighteen! (Don't laugh - maybe in another hundred years . . . ???)

[Moral education, as opposed to religious education, is something that is already being well-handled in a non-sectarian manner by competent staff in our public school system, reliant upon a wide variety of courses in the humanities. Smaller classes and emphasis on proper incentives (not monetary) to preserve and improve teacher morale will have positive impact on every child's development of their natural moral perception, Those children who do not naturally develop morally will, of course, still be in need of special education - not penal but psychobiological.]

ArtemisSmith's ODD GIRL *Revisited*

Dear Colleagues:

Because a true picture of the 1960's depends so much upon what transpired in the dark ages prior to it, I am still stuck in there trying to provide you with a transition. Let me recap and embellish:

First, by the time *The League* briefly came into being c. 1954, Itkin was already a practicing priest in the *Whatever Church*, taking Confession. Like Porcelain who seemed to know everything about everyone, Itkin immediately became the walking *Wickipedia* of the Movement. He never revealed confidences, but he ferried crucial information to which only he may have been privy back and forth and, besides Porcelain, was everyone's primary source for knowing just what was going on.

Probably the only reason both Itkin and Porcelain weren't martyred right at the start was that they were both more valuable for everyone to spy on. Listening in on what everyone was doing in those days was probably very easy, as it still is today.

ArtemisSmith's ODD GIRL *Revisited*

Of course the FBI was bugging us - it had to be. And the Mafia too. And the Mafia inside the FBI. And the FBI inside the Mafia. And other surveillance groups inside all other surveillance groups, and the Gays also inside every group.

And new technologies for spying were probably also being expanded and randomly tested. By 1958, both Taulman and I became constantly ill with the flu or whatever. Hale too. There was no let up. Was it smog or bad water, or something else? (Compare this with Martha Mitchell's account of what was happening to her post-Watergate due to what she claimed to be cancer-causing high-tech government surveillance similar to what was reportedly taking place in American Embassies in the U.S.S.R.)

All of these entities were filled with personnel whose loyalties were mixed, some pro-Gay, others anti-Gay, and a third darker element - the real *Forces of Evil* - which was gathering the kind of information that could be used for profit and extortion and would soon ally itself with the drug cartels.

This was a crowded theater, vulnerable to any shout of *Fire!* - the cancer everyone knew about, the cancer that 1950's McCarthyism and 1960'-'70's Nixonism were stupidly trying to eliminate through naïve trust in J. Edgar Hoover's demented overkill indiscriminately directed in a witch hunt against the victims rather than the perpetrators.

By the 1970's my own attempts to continue to attack the system culminated in a court case fighting to keep my academic job and bid at inclusion in a Nobel Prize awarded to researchers at Cal-Tech, blocked by

ArtemisSmith's ODD GIRL *Revisited*

closet-gays inside the cartel-infiltrated CIA.

[Look up *Morpurgo vs. Board of Higher Education NYC, et al.,* 437 F. Supp. 1135, 1137. (S.D.N.Y. 1977) and for more details also go to http://artemissmithmorpurgo.tripod.com/Consciousness.html - or wait for me to get around to writing more about it.]

  It may have been in my power at that point to provide sufficient information to rift asunder all the Movements at once by exposing double agents helter skelter who had now also infiltrated the Unions and were taking over the Rights Movements, but I did not because the end would have been selfish and the result would have been nuclear. And what if, by doing so, I too would have been playing right into the hands of the very Mob sent out to stop me?
  The old gossip-column techniques successfully used by persons such as Jessica Russell Gaver in the 1950's were no longer viable - too many good undercover people might have been killed. I preferred to remain silent and let history take its course - and that silence, too, has been terrible - but for *you* rather than for *me* - for the drug cartels took over most of the country and stole *your* childhood while I, as all sane master-builders do, turned around, dusted my feet, and went home to mind the store.
  I did however hand Judge Weinfeld a series of affidavits which might make a nonfiction novel for posterity to attempt to extract from the confidential archives of the federal courts. One courageous person therein permitted me to name her - Dr. Roberta Baker Thornton, C.U.N.Y. placement officer openly recruiting for the CIA She lived to a ripe old age. However at

least three other persons appearing in those affidavits, who were not named and were merely academic sponsors, died soon afterwards - one a suicide, the other two in separate mountain-climbing accidents. (I could never be certain then or now whether such reported deaths are real or merely quiet agent retirements.)

What were the true "Satanic" forces at play?

There really *are* persons out there with defective chromosomes, many of them crowding our prisons in an antiquated penal system still based upon false religious tenets rather than biochemistry.

Global Human exploitation through extortion and prostitution, the spreading drug and sex trade and all the moneys it provides the Mob, must in fact rely upon an army of automata, a sub-Human element that walks among us appearing to be just like the rest of us, but without Conscience, or so lacking in moral capacity as to allow themselves to be used by others.

But religion has never proved itself a cure for that. Breaking away from the Freudian tradition a new set of educational psychologists/bioepistemologists following Jean Piaget and Karen Horney have established that moral development in the healthy child occurs naturally and need not be explicitly taught.

Moral behavior is written in our genes, though some children are unfortunately born blind to it, or so environmentally deprived that their moral perception is impaired. Religious education does nothing but confound and corrupt them further. Gene therapies or other forms of bioepistemological therapies are beginning to provide a more effective approach.

But this is why we have to be ready for the future. Today, genetic therapies are becoming capable of modifying just about every character variance, including sexual preference.

The possibility of effecting genetic and hormonal changes that can also reverse homosexuality *is* still a very touchy political subject. But it *is* scientifically possible to do this now, if someone is truly feeling miserable about their present sexual orientation. (Sure, they can opt to have hormone-secreting electrodes implanted in their hypothalamus - but why bother?)

But what happens to the Gay Rights Movement when hormonal remedies become more viable?

Does this mean we should legislate a "cure"?

Does this mean that all of us with "good truly Human chromosomes" should become neo-Nazis, purifying the Human race through one or another form of gene manipulation?

Absolutely not!

What it does mean is that religious ideology needs a fix.

The whole age-old point about distinctly Human relationships is that anatomical correctness should have nothing whatsoever to do with True Love, which is Moral in type. How else will we be able to deal with Aliens, if ever they visit us, or if ever we come to recognize them as dolphins or whales or whatever other morally-sensitive intelligent life is already co-existing with us on the planet?

Matter is Matter, and Soul is Soul. (*i.e.,* How many Angels can dance on the point of a pin? Matter and Information, though they directly influence each other, reflect different descriptive modalities. Information may categorically be treated as the *Soul* of Matter.) Though no longer a question of billiard-ball cause-and-effect causality, the linguistic bifurcation is both real and necessary. The "eternal life" of Soul-infused Matter, its logico-theoretical formal structure, is preserved in *Information*. Intelligent forms recur and Moral Individuals, truly Human individuals, need to be a community guided by an ethic of evangelical *inclusion*.

True Love among Moral Individuals should be seen as architecturally neutral, capable of creative outreach and expansion, a *Love of Angels*.

We are the Angels.

We *are* the Angels and we are Moral Legion.

ArtemisSmith's ODD GIRL *Revisited*

Guys,

I think I've said enough for one volume. Go to the internet and get the rest of the story as best you can, or buy the E-books or wait for my next time capsule.

For now, let it suffice to say that the Gay Rights Movement most probably survived all the best efforts of the *Forces of Evil* to hold on to that part of its constituency because the 1950's arts pushed through the sexual revolution of the '60's and '70's, thereby making it possible for enough people to come out of the closet and stop paying off. But that took time.

A lot of time.

Itkin lived to grow out of his hang ups before dying of AIDS in 1989. By then I guess we might have rightly compared him with St. Francis, who worked among and kissed the lepers.

Attilio, until he died of heart disease in 1978, was his physician.

In contrast, Porcelain lived to a very ripe old age before probably being dumped into a nursing home in the early 1990's by one of his parolees, who told everyone he had died while on a tourist hop to Belgium.

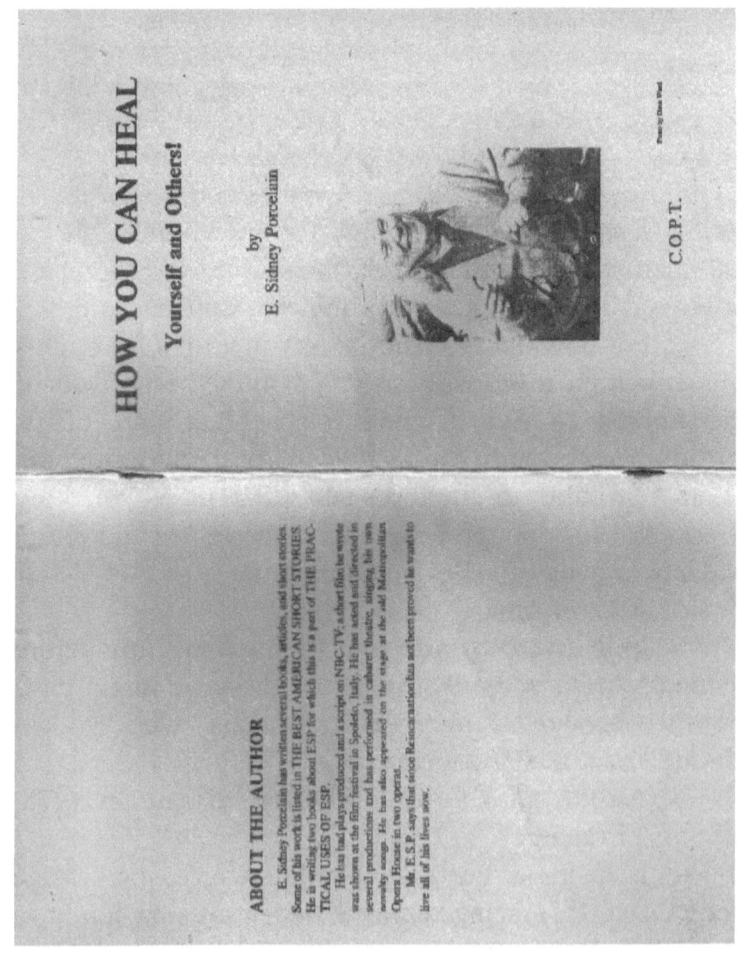

HOW YOU CAN HEAL
Yourself and Others!

by
E. Sidney Porcelain

C.O.P.T.

ABOUT THE AUTHOR

E. Sidney Porcelain has written several books, articles, and short stories. Some of this work is listed in THE BEST AMERICAN SHORT STORIES. He is writing two books about ESP for which this is a part of THE PRACTICAL USES OF ESP.

He has had plays produced and a script on NBC-TV, a short film he wrote was shown at the film festival in Spoleto, Italy. He has acted and directed in several productions and has performed in cabaret theatre, singing his own novelty songs. He has also appeared on the stage at the old Metropolitan Opera House in two operas.

Mr. E.S.P. says that since Reincarnation has not been proved he wants to live all of his lives now.

ArtemisSmith's ODD GIRL *Revisited*

Vilna died of liver cancer and TB of the brain in 1975. Before expiring she suffered the DT's and thought she was in Hell. I was there to grab my mother, look her in the eye and strongly reassure her that she was not in Hell but with me on her way to Heaven.

Billie died of so-called "dementia" and pneumonia in 2008, just a couple of months shy of her 79th birthday. By then she had acquired a whole new, though radically different turn to her artistic career.[6]

During most of those years I had been able to keep her mostly holistic and drug free, but in the end it was out of my hands - not because I was not recognized as her legal guardian, but because the pharmaceutical industry again concealed the hidden side effects of its supposedly new miracle cures.

Misdiagnosis then a stroke and pneumonia set in and she could neither move nor speak, but when I told her that we had tried every kind of antibiotic and there was no more hope, a tear fell from her eye and I knew she had heard me. I rushed to tell her one more time, as I had always repeated to her, that our life as artists and master-builders has been meaningful. That what we accomplished has been monumental.

Don't make me a liar.

ArtemisSmith **2011**

---

[6] Go to http://billietaulman.tripod.com/index.html for more.

ArtemisSmith's ODD GIRL Revisited

Coming in 2011:
ISBN 9781878998729   8x10   color illustrated   Retail: $49.95

ArtemisSmith's ODD GIRL *Revisited*

Billie Taulman in Rome, 1954.

ArtemisSmith's ODD GIRL *Revisited*

Now in E-Book and Paperback:
ISBN 9781878998347 5x8 238pp Retail: $16.95

www.ingramcontent.com/pod-product-compliance
Lightning Source LLC
Chambersburg PA
CBHW021107080526
44587CB00010B/420